POLLUTING FOR PLEASURE

POLLUTING
FOR
PLEASURE

ANDRE MELE

W·W·NORTON & COMPANY

New York   London

Copyright © 1993 by Andre Mele
All rights reserved
Printed in the United States of America
First Edition

The text of this book is composed in 10.5/13 Linotype Walbaum
with the display set in Walbaum
Composition and Manufacturing by the Maple-Vail Book Manufacturing
Group.
Book design by Jacques Chazaud.

Library of Congress Cataloging-in-Publication Data
Mele, Andre.
Polluting for pleasure / Andre Mele.
p.   cm.
Includes bibliographical references.
1.   Boats and boating—Environmental aspects.
I. Title.
TD195.B63M45   1993
363.73'1—dc20   92-43498

ISBN 0-393-03510-7

W. W. Norton & Company, Inc., 500 Fifth Avenue,
New York, N.Y. 10110
W. W. Norton & Company Ltd., 10 Coptic Street, London, WC1A 1PU

1 2 3 4 5 6 7 8 9 0

This book has been written
for my children

Tina, Justin, and Paloma

and for yours.

The bills for our mistakes
come due on their watch.

363.73
M

Contents

ACKNOWLEDGMENTS   *9*

PREFACE   *11*

1. THE SECRET SPILL   *17*

Solar Sails and a Ten-Dollar Calculator · How
Bad Is It? · Wasting Fuel · Comparing Boat
Pollution to Other Widely Known Sources ·
Social Costs · The Seas Are Turning to Deserts

2. KILLING ME SOFTLY: OIL IN THE WATER   *38*

The Bathtub Ring and the Microlayer · Oil's
Effect on Marine Organisms · The Toilet
Parable · Getting Away with Murder ·
Toward a Technology of Efficiency

3. REVIEWING THE FLEET THROUGH THE
SMOG OF TIME   *65*

The Yacht · The Role of Production Methods ·
Marketing's Influence · Racing, the Deep-V,
and the Sterndrive · The Horsepower Explosion
 · In Bad Taste · The New Rumrunners

4. GOOD ENERGY 87

Establishing the Criteria · The Rule of Capture · Gasoline · Alcohol Fuels from Biomass · Diesel Fuel · Natural Gas · Fuel Hydrogen · Solar: The Ultimate Clean Energy · The Storage of Electricity · Battery Development Today · Fuel Cells

5. CLEAN POWER 125

Wind · Invisible Refinements · Engines—From Gunpowder to Gasoline · "It Can't Be Done"—Or Can It? · Taming Exhaust Emissions · Diesel—The Dark Horse · Zero Emissions Means *Electricity* · Rethinking the Propeller · What Works

6. LOW-RESISTANCE BOATS 165

Two Fluids and an Interface · One Log or Two? · Multihulls · Displacement Hulls · Semi-Planing Hulls · Flying on Water: Part I—Planing Hulls · Flying on Water: Part II—Hydrofoils · Flying on Water: Part III—Hovercraft · Semi-Submersibles and Wave-Piercers · Defining the Efficiency of Boats · Sensible Boating? · What Works · Marine Aerodynamics

7. TAKE BACK THE WATERWAYS! 192

The Role of Government · The Role of the Boating Industry · The Role of the Individual

EPILOGUE 200

BIBLIOGRAPHY 204

INDEX 215

Acknowledgments

My deepest thanks and gratitude for encouragement, inspiration, and assistance to (in alphabetical order) Angela Boettcher, Dennis Caprio, Bim Chanler, Chris Cornell, John Eaton, Katrina Fischer, Jack Hardy, Maurice Hinchey, Chuck Houghton, Shabazz Jackson, Cara Lee, Nick Lyons, Bill Maxwell, Frank Mele, Fred Osborn, Jackie Ring, Jim Rod, Bill Rothschild, Clare Ryan, Pete Seeger, SUNY Stony Brook Library, South St. Seaport Library, Madeline Sunley, Eric Swenson, Vassar College Library, and Jerry Wexler, and especially to Jim Mairs, Marita Lopez-Mena, and Jean Wexler, without whose support this book would not exist.

Preface

A Personal Perspective

Pleasure boating, which grew phenomenally during the 1980s, has been a prime vector for introducing hydrocarbon pollution into the environment. Until now, the contamination has gone almost wholly unnoticed because it is hidden from view. The occasional cloud of acrid smoke from a starting outboard motor seems to disappear rapidly. Boats don't normally congregate in urban-scale populations, so their tail-pipe emissions don't seem obviously linked to smog, emphysema, and lung cancer. The tracks of their passing quickly dissipate, so the notion of "tread lightly," which one sees in fine print at the bottom of advertisements for other off-road vehicles, seems unnecessary for boating.

But how often in life does "the obvious" yield to some new and usually unpleasant surprise? How frequently are we betrayed by our assumptions? *Polluting for Pleasure* has been written to show how wrong we have been about the seemingly benign presence of motorboats along most of the scenic coasts and waterways of America, Canada, and Europe. The genesis of the book, however, goes back three decades.

My father was the first person to open my eyes to nature. Because he took me hunting and fishing as soon as I could tag along without being a burden, my first view of nature was in the context of survival skills. I learned to shoot when I was eight years old, and was given a shiny new .22-caliber rifle at age twelve. I could find my way home alone from the most remote areas of the Catskill mountains, build a lean-to, light a fire, cast a dry fly in silence, and clean a pheasant long before television was allowed into my household.

One day we were stalking through the forest in autumn after a rainfall, and he asked me a riddle. "Why," he said, "is it better to be hunting today than, say, two days ago?" I searched and searched for an answer, looking far deeper than necessary into what was a very simple question, and then gave up. "Listen," he said. We walked on. I listened, but there was utter silence. And then, finally, I realized what he was getting at. "The leaves are wet," I said, "and we're able to hunt without making any noise." "Took you long enough," he grumbled. So the truth often lies, literally, underfoot.

Years later, when I got out of the navy and was staying in a converted garage studio on my father's property, we spoke often about the nascent environmental movement. He was the one who first directed me to the sloop *Clearwater*, which was sailing the Hudson River as a symbolic vision of a cleaner world.

Then, in the late '70s, my father got hooked by an environmental issue, one that was particularly dear to him: preservation of endangered trout streams. He was outraged because New York City water department officials were hoarding water in their reservoirs, turning some of the best and most historic Catskill trout streams into thin, dead trickles occasionally scoured by catastrophic flooding.

He spent the next seven years in a world that was as alien

to him as the moon would be to you or me. A solitary person by nature, he helped found a group called Catskill Waters, and was soon embroiled in meetings, shouting matches, political intrigues, lobbying, and threats. After seven years of battling for legislation to establish minimum releases from the reservoirs, he and his associates won. Today the streams are never allowed to fall below certain levels, and they are viable ecosystems again. New York is finally installing water meters, the last major city in the country to do so. And my father, at the age of eighty, is out there some summer Mondays, wading in water up to his waist as he flicks a line silently back and forth with his impeccably varnished Jim Payne bamboo rod.

Hunting and fishing never gave me the kind of deep inner regeneration that they provided for my father, but eventually I found my own point of spiritual reference. After two and a half years at sea as a signalman on the upper decks of a destroyer crisscrossing the Pacific Ocean, the South China Sea, and Yankee Station in the Tonkin Gulf, I realized that despite my congenital hatred for the military elements of the voyage, the sea was my place of regeneration. I made landfalls, albeit in uniform and behind the muzzle of a rocket launcher, at places like Midway Island, Guam, Okinawa, the Philippine Islands, Taiwan, Japan, and Hong Kong. I watched whales, sharks, dorado, tuna, flying fish, porpoises, sea turtles, jellyfish, ocean sunfish, and sea snakes. I saw a waterspout, and was on deck through several 60-knot-plus blows. I watched outrigger fishermen off the Philippines and sailing junks off Hong Kong, and realized that the seas are the historic medium that links all of humanity, while keeping us separate. If you splash your hand in the ocean, wherever you may be, and make a few little waves, someday a trace of that energy, however minuscule, will lap at the pilings of a dock in Hong Kong. It's magic.

The oceans, because of their sheer mass and volume,

impart constancy and stability to our entire planet. They are by far the largest unit of biological activity on earth. They exert a controlling influence over our planet's atmosphere, climate, and the biological balance of interrelationships now known as ecology.

To poison the oceans and their tributary waterways is surely to poison the heart of our existence.

Over the years my access to the healing seas has come through my involvement with boats—designing, building, and restoring them. And yet, as a result of the investigations I conducted in the aftermath of a solar-powered voyage on the Hudson, I had to face up to an unpleasant reality: my industry—pleasure boating—is waging real war, conducting a massive onslaught, against those very seas.

We who love boats and the water are the primary users of the greatest wilderness regions on earth—the oceans, bays, lakes, and rivers. Preservation of those regions is therefore our responsibility, and we have clearly failed in our stewardship.

This book is an attempt to regain the moral authority in that stewardship.

POLLUTING FOR PLEASURE

1

———

The Secret Spill

Solar Sails and
a Ten-Dollar Calculator

I STEERED THE ELECTRIC LAUNCH close to a rocky point called World's End, and on the steep hillside to my left I could see a West Point cadet walking with his sweetheart. The entire Hudson River, flowing upstream on a strong flood tide at 3 knots, was making a 90-degree turn around those rocks, and the whirlpools, while not exactly Homeric, spun the launch 30 degrees to port, then 30 degrees to starboard. The October sky was clear, and the sun, despite its low declination, was pouring energy onto a bank of photovoltaic panels jury-rigged to the canopy overhead. The winds were light, and I was only a few miles from breaking the world's record for a solar-powered boat voyage.

A yellow digital ammeter on the cockpit floor, connected to a pulse-width-modulation motor control under the foredeck by a rat's nest of small wires with alligator clips, read a steady 10, and a Fluke multimeter propped against the bulkhead nearby gave readings that changed rapidly: 9.7,

9.8, 10.1, 9.9, 9.6, 10.2. It was telling me I had about 10 amps of power coming into the system from the solar panels, and the yellow meter indicated a 10-amp power flow to the motor. Ten amps at 48 volts DC was delivering more than ½ horsepower to the propeller, and the boat was moving through the water at 3 knots, with a nicely audible bow wave and an occasional crisp snap from the flag at the stern.

I felt wonderful. I had mastered a raw element. I had a new power, and it was light—a stream of pure photons. Light, transformed into forward motion without noise, without smoke, and without combustion.

My magic moment was interrupted by a faint sound like a swarm of angry bumblebees, growing louder and louder. As I rounded the high headland of Constitution Point, looking at fifteen miles of the river, toward Cold Spring and into Newburgh Bay, I was surrounded by a dozen runabouts cutting figure-eights and tight circles, leaping wildly over each other's wakes and hurtling like projectiles in all directions. The little boats were fast: 50 to 60 miles per hour. They were porpoising, chine-walking, and flinging themselves completely out of the water with propellers flashing in the sun, so it was hard to believe that they were under control, and when one of them flew right past me, making a screaming left turn, the rest of them followed, playing a game of PT-boat-skipper, throttles to the firewall and torpedoes primed, strafing the enemy cruiser with twin air-cooled fifties on the foredeck and fantail. I was alarmed, because as they tried to outdo each other, they were coming much too close. They weren't smiling or waving. My meticulously kept logbook listing position, speed, and meter readings for each half-hour since the voyage had begun was soaked. The meters were sprayed, and I had to stuff them under the foredeck. My sandwich was transformed into a soggy lump, no longer fit for consumption. Worst of all, the boat's precious forward motion, so carefully monitored, and so miraculously achieved, was gone as the boat plunged through an awful slop created by the wakes of my tormentors.

I remember some of the names of the boats: *Rocket in My Pocket, Nightmare, Hellrider, Terminator, Flash*, and *Foxy Lady*. I remember the names on the outboard motors too. The noise was deafening.

Suddenly they left. Like a flock of birds or a school of fish which can change direction in an instant, they dashed away upriver without any visible or audible signal. Their battle cruiser was in flames and beginning to sink, but it had radioed for help and reinforcements were on the way. My ears were ringing. The acrid smell of their exhaust filled the air, and I could see a faint blue haze. The whole incident had taken place in less than five minutes. Clearly they meant no harm. It was just good, clean fun.

With the boat settled down and moving, and the spray cleaned up, I was left alone again, and started to work through a stack of trade magazines and newsletters I had brought along, scanning the pages for worthwhile information. I was almost through the entire pile by the time I had reached the entrance to Newburgh Bay at Storm King Mountain. Nearby stood mysterious Pollepel Island, which is dominated by a ruined fantasy castle, once the arsenal of an arms dealer named Bannerman, who had made his fortune buying leftover war materials from both sides after the Civil War and then selling it back to the government, at an enormous profit, for use in the Spanish-American War.

In the shadow of that monument to good business I started on the last periodical, a free monthly magazine called *Boating Industry*. The solar-powered launch was gliding smoothly up the bay, 10 amps in, 10 amps out, the nautical hooligans were nowhere to be seen, and I knew that in just a few more hours I would hold a new world record. I found a dry sandwich and ate it happily. Light headwinds had given way to flat calm. The tide was still fair. It was a beautiful day for a world record.

Then I saw, in the centerfold of *Boating Industry*, a table with the nationwide annual boat sales and registration figures, compiled by the National Marine Manufacturers Association. I had never dreamed that there could be 12 million registered motorboats in the United States. Twelve million! And that 8 million of them would be outboards, boats just like *Foxy Lady* and *Terminator*. I tried to imagine them on the river with me. I tried to imagine 8 million *Nightmare*s. Eight million outboard motors.

The implications hit me. I dug through my damp canvas briefcase and retrieved a ten-dollar solar calculator I had brought along. I began to poke the keyboard. I tried to write the numbers on a page of the log, but it was still soaked and my pencil ripped through the paper, so I had to stop to find a piece of dry paper. Finally, I located an old lunch bag that had been crumpled away in a bench, and after smoothing it over my leg a few times it was serviceable.

I tried the first scenario that came to mind, just to see what kinds of numbers were going to appear. If, I postulated, 8 million outboard motorboats go boating once, and if the average motor is about 70 horsepower, and if they take a normal four-hour afternoon trip, and if they fill up their tanks, as I have so many times, with 20 gallons of gasoline, and if they add the requisite 3.5 pints of two-stroke lubricating oil to the gasoline, how much oil will they put into the water through their exhaust? Eight million (boats) times 3.5 (pints) divided by 8 (pints in a gallon) equals 3.5 million gallons of oil. If those boats go out just three times, then the outboard lubricating oil spilled from engine exhaust will equal the *Exxon Valdez* oil spill!

How can that be? Is it really possible? I double-checked the equation, but everything was in order. If this is truly so, then why isn't the entire world up in arms against the pleasant but frivolous sport of pleasure boating? Where is the massive scandal? After all, boating goes on year after year, and the *Exxon Valdez* spill was only a single incident.

So I vowed to pursue the matter further. I established some parameters that I would have to quantify later. Most important of all: exactly how much oil is being put into our waterways by pleasure boats? My very first guess that day, after more thumbnail calculations, was a staggering 50 million gallons per year, or the equivalent of five *Exxon Valdez* disasters. (I didn't realize how tragically low that figure would be.) How many boats of the 12 million are actually used? What is their frequency of use? What is their average motor size? What are the emissions from marine engines? If the oil spilled is as bad as I think it's going to be, why isn't it visible? Where does it go? Is it causing damage, and if so, what specific harm is it causing?

The Gulf War clouds were gathering on that day, and the solar voyage was intended to make a statement, however small, about our country's lack of a meaningful energy policy. Years ago I had been sent to Vietnam for reasons that didn't make much sense at the time, and make even less sense now. Washington was about to send another generation of young people to fight, and possibly die, in Kuwait and Iraq. Our children were going over there to kill as many Iraqis as possible, and risk their own lives in the process, *so we wouldn't have to carpool, and so that the people driving* Rocket in My Pocket, Hellrider, *and* Flash *wouldn't have to forgo one moment of their joyriding.*

What, then, are the nature and full extent of pleasure boating's unknown and largely invisible impact on our country's energy and environmental problems?

I passed a buoy that was circled on the chart—a very special buoy—the 110-mile mark. I had surpassed the previous world-record solar boat voyage. I stood and held my hands high for the cheers of the sea gulls.

A mile away, the Hudson River sloop *Clearwater* was sailing, teaching a group of schoolchildren about the living things
in the river. The smaller sloop *Woody Guthrie* was also out
in her home waters, teaching people how to sail a traditional gaff-rigged sailboat with no motor, showing them how
to read the winds, tides, and sky; to sail and still get home
in time for dinner.

There was another boat on Newburgh Bay that day. It
was a white motor yacht, about 60 feet long, heading south
at 20 knots. I could see a wide brown smudge of exhaust in
the air behind the yacht. As I was wondering what makes
diesel exhaust brown, and adding that to my list of questions to pursue, I saw the yacht turn toward me. It had an
enormous white bow wave, and a row of white, breaking
waves in its wake as far as the eye could see. As it drew
closer, I expected it to slow down to a respectful pace, but it
kept charging onward. I could hear the low, slowly oscillat-
ing throb of twin engines that are not in perfect synchroniz-
ation. I listened intently for a sign of the throttles being cut
back, but there was none. The yacht, and its brown smudge,
came within a hundred yards before the deep rumble began
to change pitch.

The yacht loomed overhead, and it squatted as it slowed
to about 12 knots, the stern settling lower in the water. The
whitecaps in its wake reared higher, and became steep, six-
foot cresting combers. (The launch's freeboard was only two
feet.) There were two people in sight: a man and a woman
on the yacht's flying bridge. I waved frantically and shouted
as loud as I could, but my words and gestures seemed insignificant compared to the onrush of that white monster. As
they passed, the man and woman waved cheerfully, and I
could hear her shouting, "Good luck," over the thrashing
of two big diesels that were probably capable of producing
more than 1,500 horsepower. The yacht was named *Good
Times Too*, and hailed from Wilmington, Delaware, which

allows owners of big powerboats to register their craft, regardless of actual homeport, for a tax advantage.

What I shouted back can't be reproduced here. The wilder my gestures became, the more enthusiastic and genuine were the woman's waves and good wishes. Then, with the distinctive hiss of onrushing water, the yacht's wake struck. The first comber was comparatively small, and the launch rode it easily. The next one broke right over the bow and washed into the cockpit, where the water was suddenly three inches deep, sloshing back and forth violently. I heard both bilge pumps turn on. The boat fell like a stone into the trough between waves, and I heard the propeller race as the stern lifted completely clear of the water. Another wall of solid water broke over the bow, and soon the water in the cockpit was six inches deep. I could feel the boat getting logy and heavy. (Later I calculated that the launch had taken a ton and a half of water aboard.) The bow was thrust clear by that wave and pointed to the sky before it fell yet again, this time with such violence that it smashed the face of the oncoming breaker and sent up huge sheets of white water higher than the boat itself. Luckily, none came aboard, but the boat had stopped dead and began to turn sideways, parallel to the waves and in danger of rolling over. I heard a loud crack from above, as the frail canopy structure holding 300 pounds of expensive solar panels began to disintegrate.

Luckily, by then the worst of the wake had passed, and the launch rode the remaining smaller waves without shipping any more water. I looked south and saw the brown smudge disappearing into the Highlands by Storm King Mountain, trailed by parallel rows of small white streaks. I watched the backsides of the yacht's wake rolling away toward shore for a moment, then went to work bailing and cleaning for the second time that day, and lashed the damaged canopy together.

What I had just witnessed was a display of raw energy

waste. The waves had been a three-dimensional expression of manifest energy, spilled out into the natural world like a shock wave by the passage of a large white yacht with two people aboard. Fortunately, my briefcase, and the solar calculator in it, had been safe inside a bench when all the action occurred. Again I did some calculating:

One horsepower is the force required to lift 550 pounds one foot in one second. One 6-foot section of the big cruiser's wake (corresponding to the launch's 6-foot beam) had lifted the 30-foot, 5,000-pound solar launch at least 2 feet three times, and 1 foot several other times, in a time span of about 15 seconds. Six feet of wake therefore embodied a minimum of 4 horsepower, times 2, because a wake is two-sided: port and starboard. Thus there were 1,760 6-foot (4-horsepower) units of wake per mile, and I could see 5 miles in each direction, so with my own eyes I was looking at 17,600 wasted 4-horsepower units surging aimlessly across the waters. Now, 17,600 times 4 equals 70,400 kinetic horsepower—almost 300 horsepower-hours—wasted on wave action alone. And wave action is only one of the many losses associated with moving boats through water.

The white yacht at cruising speed with two people aboard had traversed those 10 miles in half an hour, expending in its engine room approximately 600 horsepower-hours, or 450 kilowatt-hours. Enough energy to transport a fully loaded eighteen-wheel tractor trailer from New York City to Wilmington, nominal home of the *Good Times Too.* Enough power to run a typical American household, with its electric washer and dryer, hot showers, kitchen range, refrigeration, heat and air conditioning, TVs and VCRs, stereos and lighting, for two weeks. Or a European household for two *months.*

An hour later a deep-loaded seagoing tanker passed me on its way to deliver a load of fuel oil to Albany. The ship was easily 500 feet long, going 10 knots, and carried thousands of tons of cargo, yet it left barely a ripple in its wake.

I concluded that oil pollution caused by pleasure boats

has a companion element: fuel profligacy. The white yacht that nearly sank me could have been burning as much as 100 gallons of diesel fuel per hour, resulting in the consumption of 2.5 gallons per passenger-mile.

As a yacht designer I knew that most boats need vast amounts of energy to achieve reasonable rates of forward momentum, but I was also aware that gross wastage and inefficiency are totally unnecessary. The white yacht had achieved a prodigious feat of inefficiency—wasting fully half the energy it expended. I added more parameters to my list:

- Fuel consumption—how can it be reduced?
- Wavemaking, hull resistance, and other causes of energy wastage—how can yacht design and technology diminish those factors?
- The social issues—just because some people can afford to buy 100 gallons an hour, are they entitled, from the viewpoints of society and environment, to be burning it in a perpetual joyride?

Three hours later I had bested the old world record by 10 miles, and decided to call it a day. Once I was back to my normal routine, I set about trying to grasp the breadth and scope of pleasure boating's impact on the environment. There was no pre-set conclusion or agenda. Just inquiry, pure and simple. I certainly had no axe to grind. I have made an enjoyable living designing and building boats for almost twenty years.

How Bad Is It?

I soon confirmed that no one had ever addressed this specific issue, and that I would have to do my own calculations, but this time I gathered real numbers to work from. Here is how they developed: There are more than 12 million powerboats registered in the United States. I learned from a study by the University of Wisconsin,* the only report to examine pleasure boat duty cycles, that the average boat is used between twenty and thirty times per season. If every boat in America were used according to the lower end of that study's usage range, there would be more than 240 million boat trips taken every year; joyriding, water-skiing, sightseeing, fishing, visiting, and picnicking. We can't trust that number, however, because our country is in a particularly deep and stubborn recession, and there are boats for sale on lawns all across America. My personal observations, and discussions with many other people involved at all levels of boating, have led me to conclude that fully half the boats in the United States may be idle or underutilized. Therefore, for the sake of fairness, and to maintain a consistently understated position, let us say that the number of active boats is only half the total, and that 120 million boat trips are taken in the United States each year. How much pollution can 120 million boats generate?

The "typical" boat, according to the boating industry, is a 17-foot planing runabout, with a two-stroke outboard motor producing 68 horsepower. It consumes about 20 gallons of gasoline and 3.5 pints of lubricating oil during a three- to four-hour afternoon of operation.† That oil is poured into the gasoline, where it dissolves readily, and its sole purpose is to coat the moving parts of the motor for a few milliseconds. Some of it is burned during combustion. Then it combines with exhaust gases and passes into the environment. What is the total hydrocarbon content of an average outboard motor's exhaust?

Most outboard motors are two-stroke engines, in which

---

* Morgan and Lincoln, 1989.

† From data gained by discussions with boat owners and dealers, and from personal observations. Outboard manufacturers do not readily publish fuel consumption figures.

every upstroke of a piston must combine the functions of compressing the fuel/air combustion mixture and propelling exhaust gases out of the cylinder—two seemingly antithetical tasks. Unlike four-stroke engines, there is no dedicated exhaust stroke. Instead of having valves which open and close according to precisely optimized timing, thereby allowing fuel in and exhaust out with a high degree of selectivity, they have ports. Ports are nothing but crude holes, and the intake/exhaust process is passive. Ports can't discriminate between the fuel/air pre-combustion mix and post-combustion exhaust. Thus every time a piston travels up the cylinder it pushes some unburned fuel out with the exhaust gases, expelled into sea and sky.

How much? The only current accessible emissions data for outboard motors are featured in a technical paper* presented by employees of Mercury Marine and Outboard Marine Corp. (the two major outboard motor manufacturers) to the Society of Automotive Engineers. According to the authors, a 70-horsepower outboard spews out 1,529 grams (3.37 pounds, or slightly more than half a gallon) of unburned hydrocarbons per average hour, based on the University of Wisconsin's duty-cycle studies. That same outboard motor will consume, on average, 5–6 gallons per hour, so at the very least ¹⁄₁₂th, or 8.3 percent, of supplied fuel and lubricating oil is blown out unburned. That is one calculation. It is, apparently, very conservative.

The federal EPA's Certification Division, working with all its resources in Ann Arbor, Michigan, on the question of pleasure boat emissions, has a different figure. They round off the engine usage duty cycle to a flat 20 percent throttle setting, and their data suggest a much higher level of outboard exhaust emissions—three times my paltry 8.3 percent. *They have concluded that two-stroke outboard motors*

* Coates and Lassanske, 1990.

pass fully 25 percent of their total hydrocarbon intake, fuel and lubricating oil, out the tail pipe and into the environment.

Their conclusions arise from statistical inventories of emissions generated by "nonroad vehicles," such as construction equipment, industrial generators, snowmobiles, farm equipment, all-terrain vehicles and motorcycles, commercial shipping, and pleasure boats.* According to the EPA, *outboard motors emit 1,760 pounds of hydrocarbon material for every 1,000 gallons (about 6,200 pounds) of fuel consumed.*

The differences between my figures and the EPA's arise from several sources. First my arbitrary halving of the number of active boats during the initial model. Second, my use of the low end of the University of Wisconsin's trip count: 20 instead of 30. Third, the overwhelming majority of older, worn engines in the field that are emitting at much higher levels than the new engines tested. Sales (flow) of new outboard motors totaled 289,000 in 1991, into a reservoir of 8 million outboard boats, for an average engine life of twenty-seven years. Fourth, Coates and Lassanske point out that the test procedures they describe ignored smoke and particulates. And fifth, the procedure in Coates and Lassanske presumed that a steady-state operation of the tested motors would best approximate the field applications of outboard motors. Steady-state operation results in as much as one-third lower emissions, but does not occur in the field on any but the glassiest calm days, in the hands of extremely tranquil pilots. Given these discrepancies, and the unlikeliness of obtaining precise figures, I fell fully justified in citing emissions calculations based on the EPA input.

If 8 million outboard motorboats (two-thirds of all recreational craft) are making 80 million trips (two-thirds of all boating trips), and consuming an average 20 gallons per

* EPA, 1991.

trip, the total of fuel consumed by outboard motors is 1.6 billion gallons. Quantities of unburned gasoline and other hydrocarbons somewhere between 133 million gallons (8.3 percent of 1.6 billion) and 400 million gallons (25 percent of 1.6 billion) are therefore being exhausted into the water and dispersed by violently turbulent propeller wash. And when we factor in the remaining 4 million pleasure boats that are powered by more efficient inboard and sterndrive engines, the total fuel consumed by recreational boats rises to 2.4 billion gallons per year. The resulting emissions rise too:

The total agglomerate oil and hydrocarbon pollution caused by pleasure boating is 420 million gallons per year.

Injected directly into the most scenic and elegantly productive ecosystems in America. Our national pride and joy.

That is the equivalent of as many as forty Exxon Valdez *disasters every year*—all the more dangerous for being an invisible spill. Nobody is confronted by a gummy, tarry, or iridescent slick, so nobody does anything about it; thus it is maintaining a constant and unremediated stress on the biota of those waterways.

How much oil is 420 million gallons of refined hydrocarbons? It is 56 million cubic feet. It has far greater toxic value than the 700,000 tons of crude oil* spilled annually that are known and demonstrated to be inexorably killing the Mediterranean Sea.

Wasting Fuel

And what about the companion element to oil pollution: fuel profligacy?

Fuel consumption creates residual hydrocarbons. Hydrocarbon pollution will exist as a function of the quantity of

* Bryson, 1992.

fuel being burned, but we know that it can be modified through applied levels of mechanical efficiency and hardware technology. Efficiency is a ratio of benefit derived to effort expended. How much benefit does a pleasure boater derive from a gallon of fuel?

Large motorboats, typically from 40 to 60 feet long, often carrying only two or three people, will burn from 50 to 100 gallons per hour while out on cocktail cruises or sport fishing trips. There are more than 250,000 boats of this size in the United States. At designed operating speeds, such boats move people along the water at a cost well over one gallon per passenger-mile. Is there any other form of transportation more profligate? Walking, for the sake of comparison, requires less than 200 calories—one-third of a Big Mac—to fuel the human body for a journey of one mile. Only a fighter jet, consuming over 600 gallons during half an hour of supersonic combat flying, might get worse mileage than a large pleasure boat.

Even small runabouts, going 50 or 60 miles (usually in exhilarating circles and figure-eights) on 20 or 30 gallons of fuel, are traveling only 2–4 miles per gallon of fuel consumed. Compare this with a national average of 20.5 miles per gallon for all passenger automobiles on the road in 1989,* and 27 miles per gallon for the 1991 model year.

Comparing Boat Pollution to Other Widely Known Sources

We can readily see, based on all the above observations, that pleasure boating may account for more than its fair share of our nation's pollution output. Despite the overwhelming amounts of oil and hydrocarbons discharged, we cannot see or smell most of the low-level hydrocarbon

* DOE, 1991a,b.

emissions in our waterways, and since boaters don't normally cluster in urban concentrations (although there are some notable exceptions) that create grossly obvious air pollution, how can we grasp the magnitude of unwanted hydrocarbon output from boats?

There is one way: by numerical comparison with automobiles. For decades, boats have been designed to operate like cars, look like cars, and to have the same basic propulsion systems. There is one key difference, however: boat manufacturers have never been subject to emission laws such as those that carmakers have had to face for twenty years. How does boat pollution compare with the widely studied pollution from cars and other road vehicles?

Apart from outboard motors, the most popular pleasure boat propulsion system is the gasoline-powered inboard, which sends power to a propeller underwater through either a shaft and strut or a stern drive. The typical marine inboard is an old-fashioned V-8 or V-6, naturally aspirated (that is, not turbocharged), and not equipped with fuel injection, electronic ignition, a catalytic converter, or any of the other emission-reducing devices now used in most cars. As primitive as such engines are, they emit only 7 percent ($1/14$th) of the quantity of hydrocarbons found in the exhaust of a two-stroke engine.* Automotive pollution controls, which we now take for granted, reduce this figure tenfold,† so that, horsepower for horsepower, a car emits only $1/140$th of the hydrocarbons to be anticipated from a boat powered by a typical two-stroke outboard motor.

The average boat is therefore a very prolific polluter. By comparing emissions on a horsepower-to-horsepower basis, 8 million outboard-powered motorboats with an average of 70 horsepower can pollute as much as 784 million cars with an average of 100 horsepower. Four million inboard-pow-

* Coates and Lassanske, 1990; French, 1990; Milliken and Lee, 1988; DOE, 1991a,b; Honda, 1991; Pelz et al., 1990.

† Pelz et al., 1990; French, 1990; SCAQMD, 1990; Dempster et al., 1990.

ered motorboats with an average of 160 horsepower can pollute as much as 64 million cars with an average of 100 horsepower. *The average pleasure boat, from interpretation of these figures, unleashes 70 times more hydrocarbons per gallon of fuel consumed on the environment than the average car. Thus, every gallon of fuel diverted to pleasure boating has a long, long shadow, looming as large, environmentally speaking, as 70 gallons of fuel pumped into a road vehicle.*

According to the American Public Transit Association,* a typical American commuter car, locked in traffic and going nowhere much of the time, emits 130 grams of hydro carbons per 100 passenger-kilometers. Most of those cars carry only one passenger. The American outboard motorboat takes 4.4 hours to travel an average 100 kilometers, and thus emits 6,700 grams of hydrocarbons to travel the same distance.

And one hour of pleasure boat operation is equivalent to more than 700 miles in a car.

To bring the point home with still more clarity, let us invent a new unit of pollution—an easily recognizable benchmark against which we can readily grasp the cumulative effects of pleasure boat emissions. What can that unit be?

Los Angeles. As in, "How many L.A.s of pollution do the boats in *your* state put out?"

In 1987, the 7.9 million cars and light utility vehicles that operate in Los Angeles, hundreds of square miles with America's most notoriously polluted air, made 29,200,000 trips per day, for a total of 10.6 billion vehicle trips per year, and an accumulation of 87.6 billion miles traveled.† On the basis of the 1987 national average fuel mileage, which was 19 miles per gallon,‡ the Angelenos burned 4.6 billion gal-

* Cited in Lowe, 1990.
† SCAQMD, 1990.
‡ DOE, 1991b.

lons of fuel that year, compared to the nation's pleasure boaters who used 2.4 billion gallons.

So it would seem as if boating should generate about half as much pollution as all the driving activity in Los Angeles. Right?

Wrong.

Remember, boat propulsion systems have no pollution-control devices. Therefore, to make a true comparison, we must multiply one-half (half as much gasoline burned by boaters as by L.A. cars) Los Angeles's worth of pollution by the "shadow" factor of 70—one gallon of gas consumed by a boat producing as many hydrocarbon emissions as 70 gallons burned in a car.

Boating in America, therefore, produces approximately 35 times as much pollution per year as all the driving activity of the Los Angeles basin, our country's most visibly polluted area.

Social Costs

The costs of cleaning up the *Exxon Valdez* oil spill have run far beyond $1 billion—more than $100 per gallon. And the bill for lawsuits and long-term effects hasn't come in the mail yet.

But the *Exxon Valdez*'s 10 million gallons was probably no more than 1 or 2 percent of the total hydrocarbon pollution received by the world's waters in 1989 from normal tanker and barge operations, atmospheric fallout, industrial effluent, highway runoff, and a host of other sources (including pleasure boats), and much less than that percentage of the hydrocarbons we put into the earth's atmosphere through the combined vectors of combustion and evaporation.

We can't even begin to calculate the costs that society would have to bear for an ultimate cleanup, à la *Exxon Val-*

dez: a removal or elimination of oil from the whole global environment. It can't be done. We can only discuss the issue, and speculate on the *ongoing* costs, the money we pay to alleviate the *effects* of pollution.

How does the pollution caused by pleasure boating look on a national scale? Motorists in the United States burn 355 million gallons of gasoline per day.* Boating, then, annually uses as much gasoline as all the country's drivers use in about a week. But to quantify the pollution caused by the burning of that fuel in outboard motors and free-emitting in board engines, it must be multiplied by the shadow factor of 70. The pollution is thus equivalent to 469 days' worth—1.25 years—of driving and fuel consumption by automobiles in the United States. (Or, from a different direction, since cars use 129.6 billion gallons per year, and boats burn 2.4 billion, then cars use 54 times more fuel, but since boats emit 70 times more pollution per gallon they are producing 1.29 times as much total pollution as automobiles.) Since trucks and buses account for an additional 20 percent of fuel consumption beyond the automotive total,† it is safe to conclude:

Pleasure boating produces as much hydrocarbon pollution as all the cars, trucks, and buses—all the road vehicles—in America.

And since road vehicles are acknowledged by most sources to consume 60 to 70 percent of the country's total energy derived from crude oil, which in turn is half the total of fossil fuels (hydrocarbons) consumed, *pleasure boating may very well share an equal responsibility with road vehicles for 35 percent of all the hydrocarbon pollution emitted in America today,* and the secondary effects of that pollution, such as smog and acid rain.

* DOE, 1991a.
† Ibid.

I have talked about the long shadow cast by each gallon of gasoline used for recreational boating. The shadow gets longer still if we consider the route by which that gasoline arrives at the pump. It takes one supertanker of imported crude oil every 41 hours to slake pleasure boating's thirst for fuel—more oil than is needed to supply many of the world's nations.

Since a percentage of all the petroleum in shipment at any given moment (and so by definition at risk) is destined for pleasure boats, it is fair to say that the true pollution caused by pleasure boating actually exceeds the figures I have been presenting.

For every gallon of petroleum product consumed, there is a burden referred to as the "social cost," and many experts* estimate its value from a low of $3.00 to a high of $5.25 per gallon of gasoline. It includes the costs society at large must pay to deal with tanker and barge spills, water treatment, the evils associated with acid rain, infrastructure deterioration, enforcement and bureaucracy, medical treatment of skin and respiratory diseases, a host of air pollution–related problems, and the military actions needed to protect politically vulnerable supplies.

We suffer these social costs in the form of higher basic taxes, a proliferation of issue-and-item-specific taxes, interest payments on the national debt and myriad bond issues, higher insurance rates, spiraling legal and medical costs, the expense of fighting an occasional war, foreign aid, and the corresponding steady deterioration of the things our money is supposed to be paying for: education, roads, health, and safety.

* Steger and Bowermaster, 1990; Morris, 1991; French, 1990; NSEA, 1990; Lazare, 1991.

The Seas Are Turning to Deserts

Who is to blame for all these woes? Not industry, or plea-sure boating per se. As a Greenpeace-sponsored advertise-ment stated shortly after the *Exxon Valdez* accident, in a caption under Captain Hazelwood's photograph, "It wasn't his driving that caused the Alaskan oil spill. It was yours."

Like most pollutants, oil in the water is the result of an economic policy based on perpetual growth, which, like perpetual motion, goes against the most basic laws of nature. It masks the rapid depletion of finite resources and encour-ages the rapid disposal of slightly used goods. We are told by our politicians and economists that we must go on like this forever, discarding and repurchasing in ever-shrinking aging cycles, or the balloon will collapse. While economies grow, however, the natural capital of the geosphere and the biosphere cannot grow apace—in fact they can only dimin-ish in both scale and quality. As the proportion of man-made substances to natural substances rises worldwide, the system becomes stressed. Oil in the water is a tragic embod-iment of that stress.

Oil floats to the surface of water, as everyone knows, and has unbelievably far-reaching implications affecting 80 to 90 percent of all aquatic life.* It affects the vital exchange of atmospheric gases between the oceans and the air, and may have the capacity to alter long-established weather patterns. As we are about to learn, the uppermost inches of all wilderness waters play host to an astonishing array of life: to the eggs and larvae of most fish and shellfish, and to the plankton that most fish depend on for food. Copepods, the most abundant multicelled organisms on earth, inhabit that region. Chronic low-level oil contamination is known to diminish or even destroy the reproductive success of entire

* Hardy, 1991; Rod, personel communication, 1992.

marine populations. This in turn jeopardizes the creatures that feed on them, and places the entire food chain at risk. Oil in the water goes right to the heart of life as we know it.

How much damage has already taken place?

Yachting magazine recently published observations from a number of competitors in the 1990 BOC Challenge, a single-handed sailing circumnavigation. In a column titled "Are the Seas Turning to Deserts?"* the sailors spoke from their unique water-level perspective, their sustained and wide-ranging contact with the seas, and the contemplative solitude each is afforded, so different from the point of view of a tanker captain or a crewman aboard a military vessel. Listen to their words, as we temporarily exit boats and enter biology to learn *why* oil in the water is so bad:

> . . . most noticeable was [the ocean's] eerie lifelessness. I saw no birds, and no sea life . . .

> The seas are almost empty of wildlife, and only idiots like us who sail the oceans seem to be noticing it.

> There has been a massacre out there. The seas are turning to deserts.

* Pickthall, 1991.

2

Killing Me Softly: Oil in the Water

AFTER QUANTIFYING THE MAGNITUDE of oil pollution caused by pleasure boats, several questions remained unanswered, and became the basic parameters of a second level of inquiry:

- Where does that oil go?
- Why can't we touch it, see it, or smell it?
- We sense that oil in the water is a bad thing, but do we really know why?

We are accustomed to seeing photographs of oil-soaked cormorants and the tar-slicked corpses of seals, and thus judge, by simple association, that oil is bad. But if the cormorants appear to be normal, and the seals are swimming in what appears to be clean water, does a problem really exist? Maybe the oil simply "disappears," as some studies have suggested.

I realized that in order to find answers to these and many other questions, I would have to find the trail of those 420

million gallons of oil, and follow their path through the
environment.

The Bathtub Ring
and the Microlayer

I have been using the terms "oil" and "hydrocarbons" as
if they are synonymous to avoid confusing some readers who
are not schooled in this specific technical field. But people
who have been trained in this discipline will be quick to
point out that there is a difference. Not in the big picture,
perhaps, but in the mosaic of small facts which make up the
big picture. Understanding the difference will help us to
understand the problem.

Oil contains hydrocarbons, but hydrocarbons are not oil.
Hydrocarbons are hundreds of distinct chemical compounds, and oil is the more viscous and noticeable substance they comprise. Oil, furthermore, can be anything from
thick, tarry crude oil to watery No. 2 home heating oil and
diesel fuel, which are much more volatile and much more
toxic. Different types of oil behave differently in water, and
as a function of varying temperatures and climatic conditions. Oil cannot become airborne, unless temporarily as a
fine spray.

Hydrocarbons can be gaseous, liquid, and even solid, as
ash. The exhaust of a two-stroke outboard motor will indeed
have oil in it, from unburned lubricating oil—some 50 million gallons of it every year. But it will also contain a staggering array of hydrocarbon compounds, some of which were
carried from the gasoline, through combustion, and into the
exhaust more or less intact, and some of which were created
in the crucible of the engine's cylinders during combustion
from compounds in the gasoline.

Hydrocarbons and oil do not accumulate in mountains,
like plastic or most other forms of solid waste. Oil pollution

caused by boats is spread thin, and is mostly composed of the less visible and more volatile hydrocarbons, and since our nature is to ignore that which we cannot readily see, it becomes an abstraction, requiring by definition an act of the intellect to perceive it.

That may help explain why it took a wet and angry boat designer with a ten-dollar solar calculator to initiate the process of recognition.

The pleasure boat problem is not creating individual hell-holes like Prince William Sound or the Burgan oil field in Kuwait, where black oil coated everything for miles around with toxic, life-suffocating ooze. There are no jets of flame blasting hundreds of feet into a blackened sky and roaring, as I was told by a Kuwaiti friend, "like a thousand F-111s at takeoff thrust." In darker moments I visualize the problem more as a vicious little secret, kept in the boardroom among industry conspirators who don't want to defile the saleable image of bright, perky motorboats dancing in a white froth over the sparkling waves, flags snapping crisply in the wind, girls in bikinis grinning toothpaste smiles and waving gaily.

What is actually happening, then? What is the true nature of boat-propagated oil and hydrocarbon pollution?

On average, 35–40 percent of it stays in the water,* and the rest evaporates into the air. The 60–65 percent that evaporates immediately joins all the atmospheric pollutants that we know quite well. We know that evaporated hydrocarbons are the most toxic kind, and that they are firmly linked to various ailments such as cancer and emphysema. We know that hydrocarbons link chemically with oxides of nitrogen in a complex chemical process, including photo-reactivity under sunlight, to form smog, a familiar and harmless-sounding name for a truly awful substance no one would want to breathe if they had a choice. We also know

---

* EPA, 1991; Coates and Lassanske, 1990, citing Southwest Research Institute.

that hydrocarbons link up with sulfur oxides to form acid rain. These phenomena are, if imperfectly understood, the subjects of tremendous study, research, and social initiatives.

Not so the water pollution.

Assuming that the EPA's oil and hydrocarbon emission figures are correct, 37.5 percent of 420 million gallons—157,500,000 gallons—remain waterbound. Added to that figure would be a significant, but unquantifiable, additional return of hydrocarbons to the water in the form of atmospheric fallout. According to Dr. John Hardy,* at Western Washington University most post-combustion hydrocarbons are associated with or chemically bound to solid particles, which makes them heavier than true evaporatives (gases), and more likely to descend upon cooling in the immediate area, or to attract droplets of moisture that fall as rain later. That fallout would join the other components of waterbound hydrocarbon pollution, such as industrial wastes and road runoff caused by blacktop leachate, tire residue, and vehicle exhaust.

No one knows the actual percentages or quantities of these pollutants because they vary infinitely depending on terrain, climate, and population. This book is the first known attempt to quantify just one element of the entire system. Scientists have, however, studied individual elements (the mosaic pieces) of hydrocarbon-contaminated water, most of them saltwater studies, with a high degree of sophistication. While it is possible that fresh water may respond to hydrocarbon contamination inconsistently with salt water—and because of its low mineral content be able to hold more contaminants in solution—saltwater studies are all we have to work with.

---

* Hardy, personal communication, 1992.

A team of scientists from the Woods Hole Oceanographic Institute* has been maintaining an ongoing study of the 1969 West Falmouth (Massachusetts) oil spill. Back while we were bombing Haiphong, the coastal barge *Florida*, carrying a load of No. 2 home heating oil, ran aground on a rocky ledge in Buzzards Bay and poured 168,000 gallons into the surrounding waters. The wreck is still there. I've sailed past it dozens of times.

Woods Hole is only a few miles away from the wreck site, so the biologists inherited their very own oil spill to study. Twenty years after the event, they have issued a report that is the result of studies into the long-term effects of one cataclysmic incident.†

Number 2 fuel oil is a refinery product, and is comparable to diesel fuel. It is loaded with hydrocarbon compounds called toxic aromatic low-boiling fractions, or bicyclic and tricyclic aromatic hydrocarbons. These polycyclics include chemicals like benzene, hexane, diethylphthalate, disobutylphthalate, dibutylphthalate, diethylhexylphthalate, napthalene, methyl-napthalides, biphenyl, acenaphthylene, acenaphthene, fluorene, phenanthrene, fluoranthene, pyrene, 2,3-benzofluorene, tetramethylated dibenzothiophenes, and many, *many* more.‡

These compounds are present in crude oil, but reach higher concentrations in refined hydrocarbons. The higher the degree of refinement, the greater the concentrations of *polycyclic aromatic hydrocarbons (PAH)*. Thus gasoline, the primary boating fuel, has more PAHs than diesel fuel, and kerosene, No. 2 fuel oil, and jet fuel have more than crude oil.

There are two reasons to fear PAHs: First, they are muta-

* Hampson, personal communication, 1992; Tripp, personal communication, 1992.

† Teal et al., 1992.

‡ Berthou et al., 1987; Cross et al., 1987; von Westernhagen et al., 1987; Hardy et al., 1987b.

genic (causing mutations), morphogenic (causing physical deformations), carcinogenic (causing cancerous growths), and teratogenic (producing fetal malformations, from a Greek root word meaning "monster").[*]

Second, they are the most persistent components of sea-surface oil contamination. Despite their volatility, they will combine with water in solution for long periods of time, as water-soluble fractions,[†] and accumulate in living tissue, building to lethal concentrations as the tissue is passed along the food chain.

In fact, of the approximately 1 percent of spilled crude oil that does dissolve, 50 percent will typically be PAHs. The toxic effects of 10 parts per million (ppm) of dissolved fuel oil, which is a potentially lethal level of contamination for many microorganisms and for some larger creatures over a long term, can be matched by 50 parts per billion (ppb) of dissolved PAHs, a very low, and as we will see, quite common level.

Therefore, the comparatively tiny West Falmouth spill killed everything in its path for a few days, and then "disappeared." Of course, nothing really disappears; it just goes somewhere else. In the case of a spill like West Falmouth, the oil evaporates, photo-oxidizes, drifts away, sinks into the sediments, dissolves in the water, filters its way into tidal regions, and is absorbed by the biota (living organisms) of the area.

Twenty years later, most of the deep-water oil deposits which had spread over 4,000 acres, killing bottom flora and causing significant erosion, seem to be gone, but ashore in the tidal marshes where it was washed by onshore winds back in 1969 it is still very much present. The biologists' core holes immediately filled with oily water once the samplers were removed. The mussels are still contaminated with

[*] Hardy et al., 1987b.
[†] Corner et al., 1983.

oil. Marsh-dwelling fish are still tainted with oil, as are the crabs. Below a depth of five inches in the tidal muck, oil persists despite being washed twice a day by the tide, 365 days a year, for twenty years*: 14,600 cycles of Mother Nature's washing machine. Oysters removed and placed in clean water for six months were still unable to get the oil out of their systems. Suspicious reductions in local bird populations have been noted also, but the scientists, always circumspect, won't pass judgment.

Oil collects and accumulates in other tidal marshes as well.† Just as soil from a human body will collect around the waterline of a bathtub, so will the most minute quantities of oil collect around the edges of a waterway. It can be seen on the stalks of marsh plants, and it can be smelled in the tidal mud. It can be found in the flesh of marsh-dwelling organisms.

Unfortunately, in both saltwater and freshwater environments, these tidal shallows are also one of the primary nurseries for the young of marine species.

The eggs, larvae, fry, and hatchlings of 80 percent of North Atlantic marine creatures spend part of their lives in the coastal nursery shallows. At that point they are vulnerable to oil retained in the wetlands, and to the potential of mutations, cancer, and outright death implicit within the complex networks of hydrogen and carbon atoms. The Florida mangrove swamps shelter 90 percent of the mid-Atlantic marine species' young at various points in their development, and so play a role that is even more critical.‡

The "bathtub-ring" effect happens because another particularly sensitive region of the earth's surface plays host to most of the stray hydrocarbons adrift in the environment: *the sea-surface microlayer*, a chemically enriched surface layer less than one millimeter thick. Wind and wave drift toxic

---

* Tripp, personal communication, 1992.

† Rod, personal communication, 1992

‡ Ibid.

elements of the microlayer onto the continents' lee shores where they ultimately deposit and accumulate.* These lee shores in the Puget Sound area studied by Gardiner are often coincident with shellfish beds that have been put on advisory or outright closure by federal or state agencies.

The upper few centimeters of the ocean is a very busy place. Like the coastal marshes, it is a nursery zone, nurturing the eggs, larvae, and fry of most marine fish, crab, and lobster, in a dense stew of tiny shrimp, algae, bacteria, zooplankton, jellyfish, seaweed, and nutrients collectively called "neuston."† Bacteria actually adhere to the underside of the surface film. Fish eggs float, buoyed by fat globules, and some organisms, like snails, seaweed, and jellyfish, float because of trapped air bubbles. Large mats of seaweed at the surface of the Sargasso Sea are the domain of baby sea turtles. Seabirds live by feeding from the microlayer. Many fish, including the enormous whale shark, depend on great quantities of sea-surface water that they strain for nutrients. Many fish migrate upward from ocean depths to feed on the surface. The microlayer thus forms the base of an extensive food chain.

But, according to Dr. John Hardy, "A polluted surface microlayer has the potential to poison much of the complex food web, including fish, crustaceans, whales, and seabirds." Oil floats, and thus concentrates at the microlayer—the worst possible place—where marine life forms are smallest, youngest, and most vulnerable. Contaminated microlayer samples have been taken from every ocean, even in the most remote regions of the planet. Hydrocarbons found in the ocean microlayer far from shipping lanes are primarily replenished by atmospheric fallout—some of it from pleasure boats, much of it from industrial and other sources. Closer to the shipping lanes there are visible slicks from

* Gardiner, 1992.

† Hardy, 1991; Hardy et al., 1987a.

tanker discharges, and in proximity to coastal population centers there are higher concentrations of hydrocarbons from land runoff.

"Destruction of the microlayer," continues Dr. Hardy, "may even alter the exchange of gases between the atmosphere and the ocean, thereby affecting global climate." Phytoplankton at the surface release a sulfide gas that carries droplets of sulfur into the atmosphere, and cloud mists are formed around the droplets. Their density determines how much sunlight will reach the earth. It would not be unreasonable to contemplate oil pollution at the oceans' surface becoming extensive enough to interfere with the exchange of carbon dioxide and oxygen between the oceans and the atmosphere that is so basic to life on the planet.

Somewhere inside us we must all be getting the same subconscious message when we see the dying creatures in Prince William Sound or the Persian Gulf: we are seeing a glimpse of a terrifying future.

Coastal marshes and other intertidal environments, the sea-surface microlayer, and the creatures that inhabit them are the target and repository for most waterborne hydrocarbon pollution, including that from pleasure craft.

Bulk water samples (below the surface) have consistently shown little evidence of oil contamination from pleasure craft.* There is a different story at the surface, however. Chmura and Ross say, "Once exhausts are released into the water, some hydrocarbons become suspended in the water at propeller depth, while others concentrate at the surface, where they may evaporate."† Do they evaporate?

Berthou et al.,‡ in their studies of the Amoco Cadiz disas-

---

* EPA / BIA, 1975; Milliken and Lee, 1988; Chmura and Ross, 1978; von Westernhagen et al., 1987.

† Chmura and Ross, 1978.

‡ Berthou et al., 1987.

ter on the north shore of France, found that oysters in the area were profoundly contaminated with aromatic hydrocarbons seven years after the event occurred. The oysters studied were two to three years old, and hadn't even been born at the time of the wreck, but contained levels of PAHs 2,000 to 4,000 times above those of "normal" open Atlantic oysters, far from the site and remote from shoreside population densities. The researchers also noted mortality rates as high as 50 percent above normal.

Commenting that long-term oil persistence is greater in low-energy (cold-water) environments, the report states that more than seven years after the wreck, the gradual decrease in the oysters' oil contamination "was characterized by an initial rapid loss of the more hydrosoluble normal alkanes and light aromatic hydrocarbons and the persistence of polycyclic aromatic hydrocarbons." The writers also say that *"these compounds are the most persistent in the marine environment and may present a potential risk for human health* [italics added]."

Corner et al.* state that "more of these compounds [hydrocarbons] are present in the 'dissolved' form than as particulate material."

We tend to measure the degradation of our environment against a pristine ideal circumstance, with clean sparkling water and smiling scallops, as if we could put it all back again, undoing all the damage that has been done. Berthou et al. and Widdows et al.† did studies to see how long it would take for a variety of organisms to shed themselves of their hydrocarbon burden in a clean environment. Berthou assumed that certain relatively clean areas were "zero" for the sake of his oyster research. Widdows took his mussels to the laboratory to create his own clean environment. But is this relevant to the real world?

---

* Corner et al., 1983.
† Berthou et al., 1987; Widdows et al., 1987.

In the natural environment, with constantly replenished or increasing levels of hydrocarbon contamination, when exactly are organisms going to enjoy the opportunity to detoxify? Considering the massive spill (six times the 70 million gallons of the *Amoco Cadiz*—but much heavier in PAHs) dispersed with uncanny equity by pleasure boats in the United States every year, it is surely correct to assume that the organisms in our country's waterways are never going to enjoy a day free of hydrocarbon contamination, especially since the organisms themselves are one of the statistical resting places, or what biologists tellingly call "fates," of oil in the water.

Oil's Effect on Marine Organisms

Marine organisms ingest oil by filtering water or by eating other, contaminated, organisms. To survive they must eat constantly. They filter contaminated water all day long, and eat contaminated food continuously. Thus, they build within themselves an endlessly replenished concentration of hydrocarbons. Kocan et al.* discovered concentrations of benzene in herring embryos 11 times greater than in the host waters. Berthou's oysters were 2,000 times more polluted than the waters they lived in. Similar effects, called bioaccumulation, have been observed in fish subjected to other toxins, such as heavy metals or polychlorinated biphenyls (PCBs), leading to a variety of limits and bans on consumption by humans.

As the toxins, hydrocarbons included, work their way through the food chain, they become increasingly concentrated. The host waters may be only slightly contaminated, but the creatures that live in them are being afflicted to a much greater degree. This is one of the keys to understand-

* Kocan et al., 1987.

ing what happens in water with constant low-level pollution, such as pleasure boat emissions.

But what does oil contamination actually do to living creatures?

We have already touched on mutation, cancerous growths, monstrous malformation, and death. Hardy, von Westernhagen, and Cross and their colleagues* have all found extensive chromosome damage in their subject populations. Kocan et al.† report larval deformities that result in grotesque growth patterns similar to those seen in thalidomide embryopathy in human infants.

Von Westernhagen finds that "pure [undiluted] Travemunde and Elbe [river] microlayer samples reduced total [turbot] hatch to 59 percent and 63 percent, respectively." He goes on to note that 100 percent of those hatches were abnormal, and that the average time to hatch was accelerated, indicating premature births.

Hardy reports that urban waters (in the vicinity of cities or high population densities) contained only 15 to 35 percent as many suface dwelling organisms as open water samples. Urban waters hosted only 1 percent of the fish egg density found in open waters during a major spawning season, thus indicating very high death rates attributable to microlayer pollution.

In his home waters of Puget Sound, Hardy and his associates found that chromosome abnormalities existed in up to 63 percent of fish embryos exposed to the contaminated microlayer. In controlled experiments, fish larvae showed normal hatches of only 4 to 42 percent of normal after only 6 days' immersion in the water samples. Trout cells in laboratory cultures showed reduced growth. Aside from outright death, kyphosis (bent spine) appears to be the most commonly recurring deformation, although other condi-

* Hardy et al., 1987a; von Westernhagen et al., 1987; Cross et al., 1987.
† Kocan et al., 1987.

tions included scoliosis (another spinal deformation), lordosis (bone malformations), deformed eyes or jaws, and defective yolk sac development.

Hydrocarbon exposure also reduces the energy available to organisms for bodily functioning and for breeding. Axiak and George* studied the bioenergetic responses of some mollusks in the laboratory by exposing them to about 30 ppm of crude oil, similar to concentrations found in many Mediterranean bays and harbors. Measuring indicators of energy intake and output, and then comparing aspects of control mollusks to oil-exposed mollusks, they concluded that "exposure led to a significant drop in the energy available for somatic growth and reproduction." The oil-exposed animals had overall bioenergetic levels reduced to 73 percent of their unexposed counterparts.

Other studies, observing copepods in an oil-contaminated environment, found that the voracious little plankton were able to process oil up to a point, measured by robust excretions of oil-rich fecal pellets.† When the oil concentrations rose to 10 ppm, however, the fecal pellets began to drop with less and less frequency as the creatures began their slow surrender to death, which occurred within twenty-four hours.

Ultimately, reproduction is the most crucial factor affected by long-term, low-level hydrocarbon contamination. An organism, in order to exist as a viable life form, must be able to reproduce itself successfully, but once deformities and high hatch mortalities become a factor, that ability, and thus life itself, is gravely threatened.

Hardy says, "We are all familiar with the dramatic destructiveness of large petroleum spills, although most of the television images are of cuddly otters and birds suffering fouled fur and feathers. However, the less visible—but

* Axiak and George, 1987.
† Corner et al., 1983.

much more pervasive—chronic contamination of the microlayer may present an even greater threat to many species. Oil, spreading over the water's surface at the same time that fish are releasing their eggs, can devastate a population's reproductive success."*

Some of the research cited here is related to urban samples or areas afflicted by major oil spills, and as such may have only a general, nonspecific application to the subject of this book, although I have taken special care to use only material concerned with the issue of low-level, steady-state, long-term contamination. Three of these studies, however, involved samples that directly relate to pleasure boats.

Kocan et al. and von Westernhagen et al.† took all of their samples from marinas in cold-water north European areas. Cross et al.‡ operated from several sites in the warm waters of southern California, and found that one of their most contaminated sites was an area dominated by a large marina, with no industrial or population centers nearby.

How much oil does it take to begin causing damage to life? According to Corner et al.,§ who cite several other studies, "animals are sensitive to chemical signals at low concentrations, often well below the parts-per-billion range, and may rely extensively on this sensory input to control their attitudes and behavior." This is the beginning of the oil-contamination response; the first whiff, the first flinching, like a traffic-bound commuter stuck behind a smoking bus.

Widdows et al.‖ report reduced food absorption efficiency, reduced body mass, reduced growth, utilization of body reserves for survival, and outright death as common responses to as little as 0.03 ppm oil contamination. Smith

* Hardy, 1991.
† Kocan et al., 1987; von Westernhagen et al., 1987.
‡ Cross et al., 1987.
§ Corner et al., 1983.
‖ Widdows et al., 1987.

and Cameron* observed high mortality rates and malformations in herring larvae subjected to 0.3 ppm of Prudhoe Bay crude oil. Milliken and Lee† cite a U.N. study done in 1982 listing toxicity levels for the full range of aquatic organisms. According to that study, larvae of all species are poisoned at levels of from 0.1 to 1 ppm. Adults of the species have higher levels of tolerance: crabs and lobsters start to die at 1 ppm, and finfish start to die at 5 ppm.

Tainting, which is contamination that has imparted a smell or taste to the flesh of fish or the water they swim in, has often been used as a yardstick of pollution content. Most reputable researchers agree that tainting occurs in water at 0.33 to 1 ppm; in other words, one gallon of oil, or less, can make a million gallons of water taste and smell bad.

The Boating Industry Association, on the other hand, insisted in 1975, with the help of the federal EPA, that fish don't have a noticeable taint until 110.5 ppm is reached.‡ (It is worth noting here that the Clean Air Act has set the limit for polluted *air* at 5 parts per *billion*. Fish evidently have no representation on Capitol Hill.)

Whatever the true levels may be, *the contamination is happening*. Gardiner,§ tested the sperm and eggs of Puget Sound sand dollars (*Dendraster excentricus*) exposed to "bathtub-ring" samples of sea-surface microlayer, beach deposits, and mud, all containing a host of toxic materials including hydrocarbons. He listed abnormalities, many of them deadly, in the resulting embryos: shrunken cell nuclei, dissolution of cell nuclei, fragmentation of nuclei, abnormal chromosome configurations unable to complete their normal differentiations prior to cell division, unusual cell forms, appearance of large, undifferentiated cells in advanced

* Smith and Cameron, 1979, cited in Kocan et al., 1987.
† Milliken and Lee, 1988.
‡ EPA / BIA, 1975.
§ Gardiner, 1992.

embryo, giant cell formation, sticky chromosome bridge, stray chromosomes, lagging chromosomes, fragmenting chromosomes, bridged chromosome groups, unequal chromosome distribution, and spindled chromosomes.

Pictures of these microscopic embryos with their primitive digestive tracts deformed and hanging outside of their bodies and their leglike spicules wizened are, with just a little imagination, not that different from seeing dying children in Africa, with the exception that these "children" are American.

Looking at sketches of the cellular and chromosomal abnormalities described above is like looking straight into the beginning of the end—a picture is worth a thousand words. Our cells and our chromosomes are not that much different from those of *Dendraster excentricus* and a million other beings who share with us the same basic building blocks of life.

In fact, some hydrocarbons have been shown to mimic the building materials of hormones in insects—thereby interfering with the body's commands for growth, reproduction, and stress responses—and many scientists suspect they are doing the same in vertebrates. Our bodies flush hydrocarbons by binding them with special amino acids in the liver. If there are too many hydrocarbons for the liver to handle, they bind with macromolecules, including our DNA.*

We're kidding ourselves if we think that we are in some way superior to and beyond harm from this self-inflicted blight. At the cellular level you can't tell us apart. The message to me is: *If it can happen to these organisms, it can happen to us.*

It is clear that sustained low-level oil pollution is associated with a gradual winding-down of aquatic life. And pleasure

---

* Weiss, personal communication, 1992.

boats, without a doubt, are prime contributors to that pollution.

Remember that the damage is happening at the water's very surface, and in the intertidal zones and coastal marshes, where the youngest, most vulnerable manifestations of aquatic life are trying to grow and develop. Oil, even in infinitesimally small quantities, is inhibiting that development.

And remember, too, that marine life consists not only of adult porpoises and whales—it is also the helpless little microscopic squiggles that must grow to adulthood. They are the next generation. They represent the potential and implicit vitality of the oceans—and of all life.

But how can you measure such a winding-down process? Years and years of wildlife inventories are probably the only way. Individual species populations wax and wane in the fullness of time naturally, without the influence of oil and other pollutants, but hard data quantifying long-term growth trends of key species would surely tell a story.

In the absence of such data, however, we are left with logical projections and assumptions, and ultimately just the nonscientific choice to *believe* or *disbelieve*. Why? Because with an infinite number of sites to study, an almost infinite number of toxic substances to study, and a limitless array of climatic, geographical, and man-made variations to complicate any study, compounded by highly restricted budgets and political foot-dragging, the scientific community is in a real bind.

As I read study after study, and talked to many scientists, I gradually concluded that the scientific discipline so valuable for micro-study (small, finite elements) can hobble macro-study (global or system-wide elements—like the planet). How, indeed, can you study *everything* in depth, under the microscope and under the firmament, at the same time?

Somehow, we must. Pollution has now involved every fiber

of life, and an unimaginably complex set of interdependent relationships has resulted that may be beyond the scope of the scientific community.

There seems to be a vortex of abnegation afflicting the scientific community, a downward-spiraling ethical structure that sternly disapproves of firm, broad conclusions—publicly, at least—and prevents meaningful ideas being drawn from its noble endeavors. The results of one study, according to the ethics, should not be used even in idle contemplation of another, but must always, it seems, await yet a third linking or confirming study that is awaiting scarce funding, and meanwhile the author of the first study has gone off to do a fourth, and so on, and everything is just getting sucked whirling down into vast storage vaults of microfiche and dense scientific journals, miles and miles of them, with no real benefit derived.

Which is fine for the scientists; without those ethics pure inquiry can be colored by personal bias. But we ordinary citizens are the ultimate market, the *raison d'être* of science, and we must not be afraid to look hard for truth in all the data. They gather it on our behalf for our use, but it is not readily accessible.

And now my ten-dollar solar calculator has told me loud and clear that pleasure boats are pumping oil and hydrocarbons into the water and atmosphere every minute of every day, and those scrupulously disciplined, objective scientists have collectively told me that it is damaging many, many tiny mosaic pieces of the planet I live on. Therefore, with a lump in my throat, I state my simple conclusion:

The uncontrolled flow of toxicity must stop.

The Toilet Parable

During my lifetime I have found that in search of vision, of high-quality thinking, I have often had to look in places where the desperate pursuit of short-term wealth does not cloud people's thinking, where life does not have to be a series of linear moves—from point A to point B, and only then to point C.

There is an object lesson contained in a book called *East Is a Big Bird*, written by social anthropologist Thomas Gladwin, who studied the navigation techniques of the Puluwat Atoll seamen in search of a logical intellect system behind their nontechnological traditions.*

Most of the islanders' routine travels involve straightforward observations of the sun and stars, sea life, and wave patterns. But long voyages are a different story.

When the navigators must sail outside of familiar territory, they are not able to rely upon observational reasoning. What do they do? They imagine an island at a precise location, and then sail past it. *Using the imaginary island as a point of reference, they reach the real objective with perfect accuracy.*

In this spirit, and in search of an imaginary island, I spent a day at Scenic Hudson's 1991 (second national) Water Symposium in New York City. It was not about sea or river water exactly, but about resource water. Drinking water. The theme of the symposium was conservation, and since my theme was efficiency, I was certain that there would be some derivative parallels, and I was correct.

One of the speakers was Barbara S. LaHage, who is Conservation Program Manager for the Massachusetts Water Resources Authority in Boston. She told the story of her

* Gladwin, 1970.

institution's battle with the plumbing equipment manufacturers of America. Businesspeople are businesspeople, whatever they make or sell, and so the story becomes a parable for the dysfunctional boating industry.

Boston had decided, as many cities have, to subsidize the installation of a million low-flow toilet fixtures in the city, to help reduce stress on the municipal reservoirs. Toilets account for more wasted water than any other urban hydrologic feature. Boston went to the major fixture manufacturers, cash in hand, and said, "Sell us low-flow toilets."

The manufacturers refused. "There's no market for low-flow toilets," they said. (Sounding just like a lot of the boatbuilders I've been talking to.)

The city responded, "What do you mean? *We are the market.*"

Nobody in the corporate boardrooms seemed to understand. The companies dragged their feet for years and years, insisting that there was no market, but finally the low-flow toilets materialized. Since then, ironically, those politically correct toilets have become highly successful advertising cornerstones for the plumbing companies.

There are a thousand good reasons to have "low-flow" *boats:* low operating cost, reduced insurance (because of slower speeds and the statistical presence of electric and hybrid boats, which carry little or no flammable fuels), easier maintenance, less stress, greater safety, all-family participation, and environmental beneficence being just a few. The missing link is a demand stimulus, an Authority, like Boston or Los Angeles, that is ready to say, "I'll take a thousand," or "I'll take a million of those clean-power boats." The automakers have heard the clarion call from southern California. As the law reads, they must recast their product line to include electric vehicles (2 percent of the total) and a greater percentage of very-low-emission vehicles if they want to sell a single vehicle there by 1998.

Getting Away with Murder

But even the authors of the southern California initiative forgot to include boats in their program. What is the source of boating's remarkably enduring immunity to the current wave of clean-air and clean-water initiatives?

All roads seem to lead back to one paper that was published by the EPA in 1975.* The field work covered by the paper took place over a three-year period including 1972, 1973, and 1974. The report itself is 319 pages long, including voluminous appendices, but of all the information within those pages one nugget alone entered the operative corporate unconscious of the boating industry: *boats don't cause any pollution.* And, even more remarkable, *"scientific evidence" that pleasure boat engine exhaust actually stimulates marine life!*

That report was a rationalization to give the green light for an unprecedented proliferation of engine-driven vehicles with staggering emission levels. But how valid was the report?

It was paid for by the Boating Industries Association, an ancestor of the National Marine Manufacturers Association (NMMA), and by the EPA. But what is wrong with this picture? Would you believe a report on PCBs paid for by a transformer manufacturer? How much credence could you place upon an acid rain analysis funded by a national coal lobby? A history of the Democratic party written by Ronald Reagan? As might be expected, the report is fraught with anomalies that, if not outright refuting its conclusions, cer-

* EPA / BIA, 1975.

tainly cast them in grave doubt and render them unsuitable for any further serious consideration.

Basic assumptions about average horsepower are laughably out of date. The study that was used for reference in this case cited 40 horsepower as a maximum, typically used for water-skiing, 10 horsepower as an average for general boating, and 5 horsepower for fishing. The average horsepower-hours of pond stressing were less than one-third of what they would have to be today.

Furthermore, their assumptions about boat density were incorrect as well. Today there are many times more boats than there were in 1972.

In the analysis of the field tests, no correlation is made between days when the "big" motor was run, days when the smaller motors were run, and any short-term changes that might have occurred. Only general statistical analysis was used to tabulate the results.

The test ponds were man-made, ten years old. They had never had any oil stressing before the tests, and were never checked again, so any possible indicators about long-term effects of hydrocarbon pollution were lost. So too were any possible observations about an already-stressed environment, as most are today, being unable to rapidly clear itself of a continuous toxic infusion.

Samples were taken at the bottom, at mid-depth, and six inches below the surface. No samples were taken from the microlayer or from the shore, where oil collects.

Organism studies looked only at gross population effects, not at individuals, genetics, or mutation. There were broad-brush attempts at monitoring metabolic rates among micro-organisms, which showed reductions in carbon production, and a definite trend toward reduced metabolic activity in the stressed ponds, but these results were dismissed as insignificant after running the numbers through a statistical device called a "two-tailed paired T-test, 95 percent confidence." In fact, all indicators (and there were many) that hydrocarbon pollution might have been impairing the viability of those ponds were dismissed as insignificant.

There were no specific engine emissions data mentioned or considered in any way.

There was no attempt to quantify hydrocarbon emissions in any way.

The authors of the report admit that "the fate of hydrocarbons in the aquatic environment is still not well understood."

The authors, to their credit, cited a strong need for further study. None was carried out. The customer was, apparently, satisfied.

The two subject ponds were shallow, 4–9 feet deep, and measured 220 feet long by 100 feet wide. Each was divided lengthwise by a wall of aluminum sheeting to form one test pond and one control pond. There was a recirculating pump in each pond, the purpose of which is not clear from the text, and a compressor-driven bubbler de-icing system down the full length of the aluminum walls. No description is given of the purposes of these fixtures, or their operations.

No information is provided about the surrounding lands; about fertilizer, runoff, drainage, etc., just a disclaimer that the ponds were not spring-fed, and that they were topped off (with what water, from where, and how often, is not clear) when they had evaporated an unspecified amount.

The authors admit that the effects of bottom scouring in the stressed ponds with motors running were unknown. The fact that sampled pond waters did, on occasion, show increased populations in the stressed ponds was taken as cause for celebration, not doubt in the methodology. Organisms were clearly being stirred into suspension by propwash in the stressed ponds, and settling naturally in the control ponds.

Despite the title of the paper, *Analysis of Pollution from Marine Engines and Effects on the Environment*, no attempt was made to study hydrocarbons in the air above the ponds.

The ponds were very small, and the slightest breezes could have carried off most of the exhaust before it had a chance to settle back to the water, as it would in the natural environment. Apparently the sponsors of the report were satisfied that the hydrocarbons magically disappeared, and did not feel the need to question the matter any further.

Sampling of aromatics was discontinued during the first year of the study after a laboratory test by the University of Michigan concluded that aromatics only stay in the water for a single day. We now know, of course, that such is far from the case. It is highly irregular to change methodology in the middle of an experiment, and such a path-of-least-resistance approach taken by the authors casts doubt upon all the results. Any long-term study possibilities were also lost.

Wild differential fluctuations in hydrocarbons and other sampled levels between ponds 1–2 and 3–4, and between the active and control sides of the same ponds, indicate fundamental instabilities in the experiment's structure, which should have been cause for reassessment and possibly nullification of the entire study's conclusions. Instead, the study was allowed to stand as good science.

And, curiously, the study's full conclusions, not the abstract, were listed first, before the introduction and methodology were presented. One could be forgiven for suspecting the hand of the BIA in the proud presentation of conclusions at the beginning of their report, when standard report protocol normally places conclusions last. Someone wanted to be sure the right "sound bites" were out in front, and anything else buried deeply in a report that very few people were likely to read or question.

Where does today's National Marine Manufacturers Association (NMMA) stand on the issue of environmental concern? It does have a small token environmental committee (which has consistently refused to return my telephone calls as a concerned citizen), which may be so named for its role in adversarial response and reaction rather than for any sympathetic intentions.

What is its record? When EPA PB92-126960, a long-needed report on nonroad engine and vehicle emissions, was being prepared for publication, NMMA petitioned the EPA, unsuccessfully, to *remove* a short chapter of conclusions which contained the offending sentence: "Only on-highway vehicles, electric generation, and solvent evaporation have NOx [oxides of nitrogen] and / or VOC [volatile organic compounds—most of which are hydrocarbons] emissions that exceed those of nonroad equipment." NMMA's rationale? That the report was simply an inquiry to facilitate further study, not deserving of conclusions or recommendations. The reality? It was not a sound bite NMMA wanted anyone to hear.

NMMA also tried to insist that VOC emissions from two-stroke outboard motors were less photochemically reactive (and therefore less smog-producing) than other forms of VOCs. It did not, however, submit or provide any data to support this extraordinary claim.

One can understand their concern. A look through the appendices of PB92-126960 reveals that recreational marine VOC and hydrocarbon emissions are the highest of all nonroad categories in most coastal and many inland regions. It should also be noted that *PB92-126960 is an air study, and makes no allowance for water contamination.*

NMMA's record on other issues is fascinating as well. It has fought bitterly against "lemon" laws, thus taking a firm stand against quality, and has been successful in blocking boat lemon laws all over the country. It fights against boat licensing laws, which would require that operators of pleasure boats demonstrate competence and a minimal level of seamanship, and it has been instrumental in blocking most boat licensing efforts. NMMA's position states that licensing would be an impediment to sales and would force job layoffs. It is active in fighting reasonable boat noise controls, arguing instead for a more lenient standard that will force an absolute minimum of exhaust dampening.

NMMA has also fought valiantly to hold back an avalanche of speed limit legislation initiatives, using intense lobbying efforts based on a variety of specious arguments. Police organizations patrol most waterways now, but with toothless laws, tight budgets, and outmoded boats, they have little or no authority, and many boaters brazenly elect to outrun them. NMMA thus stands firmly behind the Wild West mentality in pleasure boating. Don't fence me in.

Toward a Technology of Efficiency

I once attended a speech by Amory Lovins, an unlikely scholar who was an Oxford don at a callow twenty-one, but speaks good-old-boy colloquial American with a Western twang. Lovins is a world-renowned genius in the field of energy efficiency, and he, with his wife Hunter, founded a think tank called the Rocky Mountain Institute.

The theme of Lovins's speech, delivered to some 300 well-heeled citizens lunching elegantly beneath the Museum of Natural History's enormous blue whale, was efficiency, of course, and the subtext of his story maintained an almost mantric tone: *technology can achieve efficiency without sacrifice.* Over and over, he said it, implied it, deduced it, and extrapolated it. Like a chanting Nichiren Buddhist or a Catholic saying novenas, you have but to wish for it and say it often enough, and it will come to pass. He showed the audience dozens of ingenious energy-saving devices for the household, some complex and some dead-simple, and rattled off a succession of enticing statistics, creating the image of an Emerald City waiting for us, if we can just wake up enough to walk through the field of poppies.

Lovins was saying, ultimately, that if our society can gain a consensus about a common goal, from whatever sources and by whatever means, we can think our way out of any environmental problem. As he told us about certain utilities spending billions to add power to their grids, while others spent only thousands to work with people to reduce consumption—both with equal results—his message became clear: *efficiency is actually the most practical and least costly solution* to the pollution-versus-energy deadlock.

When we look into the technological aspects of the pleasure boating dilemma, will we be able to agree? Will pleasure boaters be able to make a swift and economical conversion from wasteful polluters to thoughtful conservers? Or will the human and technological challenges be insuperable? We will soon see in the chapters ahead.

But first: How and why did we let things get this bad?

There is an enduring saying attributable to George Santayana from the early part of this century: "Those who do not remember the past are condemned to repeat it."

Possibly, in that spirit, our first avenue of inquiry should be into the background of pleasure boating.

3

Reviewing the Fleet
through the Smog
of Time

Today 30 percent of all Americans participate in recreational boating every year,* and many more identify themselves as boating enthusiasts, making water sports more popular than tennis and golf.† Clearly boating moves us, as a society and as individuals, for whatever reasons, very deeply.

Because of this I cannot and will not believe that 80 million Americans actively wish to pollute their waterways. If boaters knew the damage they are causing, would they still be trending steadily toward bigger engines, higher fuel consumption, and more harmful emissions while the rest of society is going in the opposite direction, toward economy, efficiency, and clean power?

It all started innocently enough.

* NMMA, 1991.
† *Boating Industry*, 1992.

The Yacht

Pleasure boating used to be called "yachting." The term *yacht* is Germanic, and dates to the 1500s. Its etymological root is a Dutch word, *jaght,* meaning hunt, or chase, connoting speed. Early usage of the word in journals and literature of the sixteenth and seventeenth centuries connects the appearance of fast chase boats, "jachts," with naval activities involving members of a nation's royal family.

Kings, queens, and their children were too precious for conveyance aboard even the strongest ships of war. Despite having rows of powerful cannon gleaming in the dim light behind their gunports, those mighty ships were floating targets, slow and clumsy, built more to stand and take a beating than to sail, and as such were subject to attack, destruction, or capture. Royalty, then, sailed in a new breed of sleek, weatherly vessels built for speed and superior sailing abilities, outfitted with stylish accommodations, but able to outrun any enemy vessel, and make port safely in any weather.

Yachts also carried vital messages and delivered key diplomats to the courts of foreign nations. There would be secret meetings and conferences aboard the royal yacht, anchored in a harbor or tidal river, far from prying eyes. When the king reviewed the fleet, it would be from the decks of the national yacht, a bona-fide naval vessel.

It could not have been long before the joys of a perfect breeze, a broad reach, and a spectacular sunset added pleasure cruising to the list of a yacht's state duties. And it could not have been long before the first race was held, whether formal or informal, between the royal yachts of rival nations. A nation's pride was at stake, and if a yacht lost, there was strong incentive to build a new, faster one. Soon the design of yachts became a science of its own. A sport of kings.

Pleasure boating as we know it began on October 21, 1816,

on a very limited scale, with the launching of a small (83-foot waterline length) square-rigged hermaphrodite brig named *Cleopatra's Barge,* intended solely for carrying George Crowninshield, Jr., a wealthy Salem, Massachusetts, merchant, to the ports of Europe for business and entertainment of clients, and for the pleasure of travel in the luxury of a private conveyance. All pleasure boats today descend from that one elegant vessel.

The American Revolution of 1776 and the French Revolution of 1789 had, despite mixed political success, opened the doors throughout Europe and the New World for social and artistic freedoms, and the trappings of privilege were no longer the exclusive province of the nobility. As the upper middle class flowered, a growing mercantile bourgeoisie was made fabulously wealthy by a seemingly endless series of wars and the burgeoning flow of raw materials from America and the Far East. All the fruits of society—art, literature, music, architecture, and wealth—were within the grasp of anyone capable enough to create or acquire them, and this climate eventually produced the notion that a fast, weatherly ship—a yacht—could be owned by anyone with the means to have it built, operate it, and keep it maintained.

Through the nineteenth century, the notion of owning large, fast, spectacular sailing yachts took hold, and later in the century, when steam engines became smaller, lighter, and more powerful, power yachts began to appear as well. By the 1880s hundreds of major yachts were afloat in Europe and the United States.

Boating for pleasure soon spread to the middle class as well. The virtues of working sailing craft, used primarily for fishing in coastal waters, attracted these more ordinary yachtsmen and soon a new genre of hybrid pleasure boats appeared, born in hard work, but bred for speed and agility.

Before 1900 the internal combustion engine was already firmly established in smaller boats, and powerboat racing was rapidly speading through Europe and America. Elec-

tric launches powered by Plante and Edison cells prolifer-
ated on inland and sheltered waters, early hydrofoil
experiments were being carried out, and the first outboard
motor had been conceived.

But the new world of technology was strangely disor-
dered, as if somebody had taken a million good ideas and a
million good applications and run them together through a
tumbler. The land speed record was held by an electric car,
the Wright brothers, soon to invent the airplane, were
experimenting with motors in boats, and the Johnson
brothers, who later built one of the most successful outboard motor companies, were about to experiment with their
motors on early forms of aircraft.

The mismatches that emerged would be, in retrospect,
almost comical, if not for the breathtaking scope of their
vision and potential. The foundations of modern technology were laid before the dawn of the twentieth century by a
profusion of individual thinkers, men no less brilliant than
Tesla, Edison, Bell, Marconi, Benz, Daimler, Otto, Meucci,
and Ford, but most of them out of the mainstream, unre-
membered.

Boatbuilding companies were started, for the most part,
by enthusiasts, tinkerers, and inventors with precious little
business sense. A thousand wonderful prototypes of the
"perfect" boat were built. Some were even functionally successful, but were ignored. Many a life's savings was wasted
in pursuit of fame and fortune chasing the will-o'-the-wisp
of the perfect pleasure boat. In fact, not one major fortune
has been made from yacht- and boatbuilding. The harsh
business cycles of boating prevented even the most successful builders from retiring in opulence. Even Chris Smith
and his family, of Chris-Craft fame, went broke time after
time as the bottom fell out of the market.

What, then, are the forces that drive development? What
magical properties must a new idea possess to succeed where
hundreds have failed before? And is environmental quality

a factor in any of this? How have we reached a point where so much harm is being condoned?

Ultimately, the key roles in boating development were played by four factors: war-driven advances in *production technology*, the dictates of *marketing*, the example of *racing*, and society's demands for *excesses of power and luxury*.

The Role of Production Methods

Low-cost production is the holy grail of boat companies. Boats are astonishingly complex and labor-intensive. Both Henry Ford and Horace Dodge, highly successful as carmakers, foundered on the rocks of boatbuilding, and Ford is said to have commented after losing millions of dollars at it, "Boatbuilding was a little more difficult than I anticipated."[*]

Much of the creative energy at any boat company will go toward cutting costs, sometimes to the detriment of the final product and the company itself. Advances in technology, however, cut costs *and* improve the product.

The needs of wartime production spurred the first big wave of boatbuilding economies—the good ones. Elco made history by building 550 80-foot MLs (armed motor launches) for Allied forces in only 488 days during World War I, and other boatbuilders achieved similar miracles to meet the adamantine deadlines of wartime procurement agencies.

The techniques that were developed for war production worked equally well for the demands of peacetime, but many of the rigorous specifications mandated by defense were relaxed for recreation, and subsequent phases of cost reduction began after World War II. Wooden boats built in the late 1950s were a dying breed even before the advent of fiberglass because of poor quality.

[*] Fostle, 1988.

Fiberglass as a boatbuilding material was the single most significant development in the history of boat production, and soon boating was within reach of most Americans. The first fiberglass boats were rotproof and bulletproof, and most of them are still around forty years later. But all too soon the cost-cutters went to work, and they have not stopped to this day. Assembly procedures have been "refined," and component quality has sustained an endless decline. If improvements occasionally make it past the Scylla and Charybdis of American corporate inertia and into the production line, allowing a better boat to be built, it is only because they save money in the process.

The history of pleasure boating could in fact be written in product failures: fittings that break, ports that leak, keels that fall off, wires that turn green with corrosion, steering that fails, propeller shafts that snap, undersized or inferior winches, pumps that fail, compasses that read 50 degrees out of line, berths that are too short and too narrow, instruments that fail, water tanks that leak, gas tanks that leak, bulkheads that come loose, bulkheads that punch through the side of the boat, cleats that pull out, lines that snap, cables that break, switches that fly apart, wires reversed, masts that fall down, engines that shake themselves apart, bottoms that are split open by normal wave action, below-specification speeds and handling, toilets that clog, galley stoves that catch fire, decks that leak, batteries that go dead, whole boats that twist and deform in normal sea conditions, windows that craze and fog over, fabrics that mildew, upholstery patterns that make people seasick, interior floors that are smooth and slippery, iceboxes that turn warm within a few hours, fuel lines that are too small, water lines that burst, and on and on and on. Any boatowner will be able to think of a hundred things I didn't mention.

There are some dubious exceptions. One well-known builder of trailerable runabouts made the discovery that electrical switches sometimes fail because they are exposed to dust and water. They decided to use a switch with a rubber boot around it. The company vice-president said, "our objective here is not just to create a boat that looks good on the showroom floor, but a boat that works well for the customer." Wonderful. After one hundred years of pleasure boating, this item was actually major news, and made Florida's *Sarasota Herald-Tribune*, January 13, 1992.

In all probability, an earlier generation of waterproof switches had been taken off the production line twenty years ago to cut costs.

The idea of a nonpolluting boat, if it has ever come up in production meetings, will have gotten the axe long before reaching the assembly floor.

Marketing's Influence

Copycat marketing patterns have been a major driving force behind marine product development. Envious of the success of the automobile, boat companies decided before 1920 to market their wares as seagoing cars. In the twenties, Chris-Craft, Gar Wood, and a number of builders dreamed of selling boats to every man in America. America was going car crazy, so following the trails blazed by the automobile seemed to make the most sense.

They built sedan tops for their runabouts that looked just like the tops of Model A roadsters. Upholstery was designed to evoke car interiors. Roll-up windows were even tried, with little success. Automotive steering wheels were used, complete with the spark advance lever concentric with the hub of the wheel. Chrome trim abounded. Commuter yachts, used by wealthy coastal suburb dwellers to ride into town every day, featured open cockpits forward, just like limousines of the day. Boat shows appeared in most major cities, emulating car shows and featuring sassy women in bathing suits and jaunty captains' caps beckoning from the passenger seat. The concept of the boat dealer was also borrowed from the carmakers in a bid to win wider acceptance of the pleasure boat and sell more product. In the 1920s the Dodge brothers, who were almost as well known in connection with automobiles as Ford, built boats called Watercars and sold them through Dodge dealerships.

The boat-as-car strategy seemed to be a successful phenomenon then, and it is still heavily relied upon today. In the 1950s, boats sprouted tail fins, just like cars. Their fittings looked like pieces of Buck Rogers's spaceship, just as the tail lights and side mirrors of cars did. Today, as then, boat dealers tell their prospects that a boat is just as easy to drive as a car; easier, in fact. You don't need a license, you don't need insurance, and (wink, wink) you don't have any annoying traffic rules to obey. It's the last American frontier, where you can be who you want to be, do your own thing, and be left alone.

Creative financing of boats has also followed the lead of the automobile. Desperate to boost declining sales in the early 1980s, boat dealers offered easy financing with no money down to any living human being who wanted it, succumbing to the temptations of short-term gain. That incentive worked for a few years, but has predictably become a trap as the glut of used boats blocks the sale of new boats. Desperate financial straits now prevent builders from seriously considering investment for any purpose as abstract as environmental beneficence.

Racing, the Deep-V, and the Sterndrive

Retail follows racing. Family runabouts resemble racing boats, and are marketed as such. What does this mean for pleasure boating as an industry? And is racing likely to foster environmental concern among its participants?

Because of the romance and glory associated with racing, and because the competitive urge is a powerful motivator, racing has continued to guide development through the age of the powerboat—even though the great majority of boatowners do not race.

Today, 99 percent of pleasure boating is noncompetitive. Few venues exist for the casual owner of a recreational powerboat to race without making a heavy investment of time, money, and nerve. Bodily risk has escalated in exponential proportion to soaring increases in boat speed, to the point where the demands of sea conditions and boat handling have become prohibitive. Only the sailing fraternity, enjoying, and indeed promoting, their public image as laid-back nature lovers, regularly indulge in tooth-gnashing, bare-knuckled nautical combat.

Big boatbuilding companies try to bring knockoffs of the custom-built racers to market as rapidly as possible, even though production boats are always a year or two behind. Still, thousands of eager buyers unable to afford the custom-built racers flock to buy the latest production boats, and dream that they have the hottest boats afloat.

Powerboat racing, like sailboat racing, was established by and for citizen competitors, but eventually became the exclusive domain of professionals. The first powerboat racers were of the inspired-tinkerer-and-enthusiast species. Victory went to the person displaying the best overall combination of boat design, engine sophistication, and driving skill. Experimentation created an endless variety of trial-and-error racecourse freaks, but as with evolution, any mutation that enhanced survival abilities tended to reproduce itself successfully, and to breed imitators which were themselves subject to improvement. A repeating cycle of epiphany and refinement.

Sometimes the period of refinement wouldn't last longer than a few weeks before the next innovation would blow away all the approbation and dried-up laurel leaves of another short-lived triumph. George Crouch, who designed a number of successful Gold Cup boats, drew an innovative hydroplane in 1912, only to proclaim it obsolete before it was launched. A Sintz engine which ruled in one event would be humbled by a Pope-Toledo in the next, and a radical new two-cycle Emerson motor might arrive in time for a race, only to be bested by one of Joe Van Blerck's creations. Twenty-six-foot boats were supplanted by 40-footers, which were in turn overwhelmed by smaller boats. A successful single-step boat was surprised by a five-step boat that planed amidships and rode on propeller thrust aft. Gar Wood, in his pursuit of the Harmsworth trophy, kept upping the horsepower ante with war surplus airplane engines until a serious contender had to have 6,400 horsepower to be competitive. Rules were developed to curtail the increasingly exclusionary costs of the sport and create a level playing field. Engine displacement was limited after 1936 to 12 liters, but speeds and costs continued to climb. In 1939, the winner of the Gold Cup was a radical three-point hydroplane with a hand-built Miller 16-cylinder engine costing $100,000.

As fast as changes were wrought on the racecourse, they appeared on the general market. Most early powerboat racing was in search of raw speed, and seakeeping was not an issue, so earlier runabout hulls tended toward relatively flat bottoms and concave sections, great for skimming over flat water, but troublesome in a chop.

In the 1940s, after World War II, the glory racing went offshore. Great Britain's preeminent race was the Cowes-Torquay, most of which was in open ocean, and the best racers from America and the Continent had to do well in the Cowes-Torquay to be taken seriously. The premier American event was the Miami-Nassau race, which traversed 185 miles of Atlantic Ocean, including the unruly Gulf Stream. Inland speed racing continued, but became increasingly rarefied as the boats began to exceed, in both brute power and cost, anything that an ordinary mortal could dream of handling recreationally. Ocean racing, however, remained wide open for a time.

Today, few people pilot 200-mile-per-hour three-point hydroplanes, but millions go out regularly in boats with deep-V bottoms, a type that was pioneered in offshore racing circles, and adapted well to the casual pleasure boater.

Racers liked the deep-V because it rode a heavy chop with appreciably less pounding. The V-section spread the seas like a wedge instead of slamming down squarely. It required much more horsepower at low speeds because a lot of precious lift was spilled out to the sides by the V-bottom, but at higher speeds it continued to rise out of the water, needing less power than traditional forms, and the easier ride meant that higher average speeds could be sustained. Average speed won races. Furthermore, the relatively easy ride meant that a smaller boat could be successfully campaigned, at less cost, in sea conditions that would have favored the larger of the earlier, traditional boats. The successes and affordability of deep-V raceboats encouraged more and more imitators, and by the mid-1970s that type completely dominated power-boat racing.

Manufacturers loved the deep-V because it was easy to design, very forgiving of shifts in center of gravity, handled relatively easily and safely, which was important from a liability standpoint, and could be inexpensively tooled. Most of the deep-V boats were simply composed of four flat panels with a twist near the bow, so production tooling was quick and cheap. Lower slamming loads meant less structural stress, which translated in the blink of an eye to lighter skin thicknesses and lower production costs.

Marketing staffs loved the deep-V because of the easy saleability of any product with a racing heritage. The same characteristic that attracted racers to the type would also bring customers: a small, economical boat that could ride big seas. High horsepower numbers and big fuel consumption only enhanced the package. If a customer had more horsepower than his neighbor he was a happy man.

Oddly, most boaters are only marginally concerned about how fast they are going. Once a powerboat is planing, its passengers feel like they are flying, and the ability to sustain that sensation of splashy flight is key to the enjoyment of 1960s-style pleasure boating. Thirty miles an hour feels, to the boater, like 50 or 60, and most drivers can't tell whether they are going 30 miles per hour or 40 miles per hour. Speedometers in pleasure boats are notoriously inaccurate. Manufacturers' claims are wildly optimistic and hard to verify. Who indeed, after spending upwards of $20,000 on a new boat, would *want* to prove the manufacturer wrong? Armed with a lot of horsepower, amply demonstrated by a voracious thirst for fuel, and the manufacturer's speed ratings, the boater is content, and only craves more power or a bigger boat to make him faster still—faster than his friends.

Powerboat racing, both inshore and offshore, was the testing ground for outboard motors, which climbed from 2 to 500 horsepower in forty years. Composite construction of fiber-reinforced plastics first saw the light of day as the material of choice for building racing boats.

Another key racebred innovation was the sterndrive, in which a big V-8 is coupled directly to an outboard-like propeller unit that mounts in the boat's transom. This allowed racers to concentrate weight much farther aft than was possible with the conventional inboard power format. The resistances of the shaft, strut, and rudder were eliminated. The longer steering moment created by having a point of thrust actually behind the transom made boats easier to control, requiring fewer drag-producing helm corrections.

Emulation of raceboat drivers certainly set the stage for the horsepower explosion by glamorizing and popularizing raw speed on the water. But I seriously doubt that one pleasure boater in a thousand could name a single powerboat racer.

Builders and owners loved the new boats. They were much easier to set up mechanically, which reduced production costs, and were a snap for the owners to trailer. The pains of annual boat maintenance had been pushed forever into the past by the advent of fiberglass, and most boaters could keep their little yachts in the backyard or garage, avoiding marina bills. At long last, boat sales began to soar into the troposphere.

But at what price?

The Horsepower Explosion

At the beginning of World War I, gasoline accounted for only a small fraction of the world's refinery output, but by the war's end in 1918, that ratio had been reversed. In 1912, there were only 902,000 automobiles on the face of the earth, but by 1919 there were almost 7 million (versus 30,000 boats), an increase of a million cars per year. At the same time, the war fleets of the world were converting their old coal-burning fireboxes to oil.

Britain was first, due to the insistence of a Royal Navy captain named Fisher. One of Fisher's staunchest allies was Winston Churchill, and together they proclaimed to the reluctant admiralty, "In war, speed is everything." And speed meant oil.

Fisher and Churchill were effective in converting a high percentage of the British fleet over to oil. The resulting improvement in fleet performance absolutely secured England's domination of the seas. When, on November 21, 1918, Lord Curzon, the British Secretary of State for Foreign Affairs, said, "the Allies floated to victory on a sea of oil," he was referring specifically to that naval superiority.

In World War I, the Allies used 39,000 barrels of oil per day to prosecute the war successfully. Thus it was imprinted in our collective unconscious that oil consumption and raw speed saved the world; that oil consumption, and lots of it, is good. It keeps the world turning, and our families safe and snug. During World War II the Allies needed 800,000 barrels daily to do the job—20 times as much—which only reinforced that mindset.

During the first war any notions of military chivalry, ethics, and a code of honor died on horseback in the fields of Verdun and the Argonne forests under an onslaught of soulless war machinery. In the years between the two wars, the sons of men who had died under clouds of mustard gas, torrents of machine-gun fire, and beneath the caterpillar treads of armored tanks watched the coming of Hitler and Mussolini, and saw a new generation of war machines rise from the ashes of Europe. During the economically fallow period from 1920 to 1940, the foundation science of computers, rocketry, jets, radar, sonar, and the atomic bomb was established. Oil flowed from every corner of the globe, cheaply and plentifully. By 1930 there were over 23 million cars, a threefold increase in just over ten years.

Despite America's reluctance to fight again in Europe, it was clear to many that war was inevitable, and it was equally clear that there would be no fair play, no rules at all. The victory would go to the man with the fastest ships, planes, and armies. The key to world domination lay in horsepower. The key to horsepower was oil. Lots of oil.

Technological development thus focused its attention on the most rapid means of converting the greatest amounts of energy contained in oil to heat, and thence to rotary motion, the basic motive vector of all transportation. Vehicles had to be developed that would wring the most speed out of the new motors, and the operation of these machines created a new warrior elite.

I am only forty-four, and like all baby boomers I wasn't even alive when World War II was fought, but as a child I read, spellbound, the story of Lt. John Bulkeley, who in his tiny wooden PT boat struck the first blow for the U.S. Navy by sinking a huge Japanese cruiser during the darkest days of the war. I saw movies about Patton and Rommel, and the astonishing courage of their tank battles in Africa and across Europe. I read about Jimmy Dolittle's bombers, the Spitfire, the P-51 Mustang, the Flying Tigers, and Chuck Yeager, who bagged five enemy planes in one day. I know to this day that the Spitfire had a carbureted Rolls-Royce engine which would starve for fuel if it was flown upside down, unlike the German Messerschmitt Me-109, which was fuel injected. I know that the P-40 was slower in a climb than the Japanese Mitsubishi Zero fighter, but it had the dubious advantage of a faster dive, and the American flyers developed dogfighting strategies based on that ability. I have flown a 1940 T-6 fighter trainer in a rattling 300-mile-per-hour dive, and I think I can imagine what it must have been like in a P-48 Lightning, with its distinctive twin-boom tail, diving so fast that a pilot could actually see the rushing air that built up at the corners of his windscreen.

Hundreds of newsreels lodged in the deepest layers of our minds. Scores of movies—*They Were Expendable, Thirty Seconds Over Tokyo, Twelve O'Clock High, Flying Tigers, The Battle of Britain, Torpedo Run*—starred our favorite film idols as members of the new warrior elite, cocky and fearless, while the most beautiful actresses in the world played their adoring lovers. Propaganda pieces appeared in the media from one end of our country to the other. Later, the ultimate hero of the boomer generation became our president: John F. Kennedy, himself a PT-boat jockey, not only a card-carrying member of the warrior elite, but of the de facto American aristocracy as well.

On the eve of war, in 1940, the average four-berth power cruiser was outfitted with 90 horsepower. When pleasure boating started again in 1945, the average immediately jumped 67 percent, to 150 horsepower, and it has continued steadily upward ever since. Average speeds increased from a pre-war 17 mph to 25 mph.* Today a typical four-berth cruiser can do 35 mph in flat water, but it needs 300–400 horsepower.

Pre-war boating magazines carried advertisements for a wide variety of cruisers, runabouts, and concept boats, but the traditional yachting values of elegance, grace, efficiency, and style were the foremost selling points. Since a gallon of gasoline cost as much as a complete meal in a depression-era diner, economy of operation was a serious matter. The Evinrude Motor company claimed that its Scout model would "run a full hour and a half on a single quart of fuel."† Owens Yacht Co. proclaimed its product's "roominess, livability, seaworthiness, beauty, and economical speed." Columbian Propellers would push its customers' boats to new heights of economy. While Burger Yachts highlighted soundproofing in its promotion, Fairbanks-Morse boasted that its diesels had just cut the yacht *Doreta*'s running costs a *"full* 80%." Luders Marine claimed "the safest and dryest tenders built," and Richardson's new 1938 cruisers featured "new lines for more economical speed." It paid to buy a Kermath engine because of superlative service, economical performance, and dependability, while Buda diesels for larger yachts offered compactness, simplicity, reliability, safety, and economy.

After the war, horsepower was everything. Most marine companies had played a role in the war, whether as outright boatbuilders like Chris-Craft and Elco, or as suppliers of engines, spark plugs, wire, shafting, fasteners, or any of a thousand other components. Almost without exception, these companies used their wartime associations with the victories of the mighty PT boats and other small craft to propel

* Meese, 1973.
† Speltz, 1982.

their sales efforts into the late 1940s and early 1950s. Horsepower, and speed.

With twin Hall-Scott Invaders, a "brand-new 55-footer did better than 25 mph." Correct Craft was the choice for "high speed and perfect performance." Scripps marine engines might have been "world famous for Excellent Performance," but Chris-Craft's first line of salesmanship was speed: "New Chris-Craft 22 ft. Custom Sedan, speeds to 34 mph." Packard's marine engine division, which had powered the PT boats, said, "Get the performance that *GOES*, with your next new boat!"

Many of the smaller boatbuilders had gone out of business, and with them went the tradition of unconventional concept boats. Marine manufacturers settled on a standardized mix of products. They were selling to families, but the message was clear: power, and more power.

We remain, almost half a century later, the faithful inheritors of that post-war legacy. Second- and third-generation guardians of a global society, we enjoy the fruits of our robust power technology, and have made it possible for anyone with a little disposable income to feel as if he too has joined the warrior elite.

A typical conversation among powerboaters will generally center on one thing: horsepower. OMC, Brunswick, Volvo Penta, Crusader, Marine Power, Hardin, and a host of smaller setup shops spend the great majority of their R&D money on horsepower: getting more of it, getting it into smaller and lighter packages. OMC just spent a much-publicized $25 million to refine its 150- and 175-horsepower motors, and for all that money it only succeeded in making the outboard 30 pounds lighter and 4 inches shorter, a net quantitative gain in efficiency of less than 10 percent. Fuel economy? Not even mentioned. Just a "new short-profile

Power Path fuel induction system." The prescription for greater horsepower is still this: take the largest amount of gasoline and feed it by the shortest route as rapidly as possible to the biggest affordable engine.

If the cost / benefit ratios of OMC's recent effort are going to apply equally to similar refinements of every other engine builder's many models of engine, the next generation of refinements is going to be very, very expensive indeed. And costs escalate exponentially as refinements go deeper. The engine makers know how reluctantly their technology is yielding its innermost secrets, but they continue to pursue the linear approach. It's the only way they seem to know.

There are few plans to open new lines of inquiry, and that's not really surprising. The Reagan administration, starting in 1980, dismantled every incentive on the books for developing the technology of efficiency. It almost seems as if Washington *wanted* us to be dependent on foreign oil, *wanted* to pump billions of tons of pollutants into our air and water, as if it believed that our quality of life would be improved by a showering of America's industrial effluent. In 1982 Reagan's national budget for energy conservation was $22 million—about 2 hours' worth of U.S. oil consumption at the time.

In Bad Taste

Excesses of horsepower are matched by excesses of style and taste. Despite continual complaints about the cost of boats, boaters are demanding ever greater degrees of luxury afloat. Standing headroom in 24-footers. Multiple bathrooms with stage lighting and gold-plated faucets. Mirrored ceilings and plush shag carpeting. Recessed lighting. TVs and VCRs. Enormous refrigerators in stainless steel with glass doors and vacuum sealing. Interior decorators are routinely retained by builders of larger yachts. Glass-topped tables, elegant vases and *objets*, fine art, and drop-dead upholstery from Italy, France, and Spain. Wet bars in the living room. Long, flowing drapes. Heated towel racks. Saunas. Hot tubs. Chrome. Polished brass. Coral and marble tile. Statuary. Potted plants. Glittering chandeliers. Microwave ovens. Electric galley ranges. Cuisinarts, blenders, electric juicers. Dumbwaiters.

Owners of small boats want to copy the owners of big boats, and every conceivable feature that is found on larger, incredibly expensive yachts is now being crammed into small family picnic boats. Features add weight, and weight takes more horsepower to push it along.

Any boat that incorporates an imaginative new feature spawns imitators, and each must outdo the others. I have seen good, sensible people do things with their boats that they would never do at home. Good taste seems to be left ashore at the gangplank.

In the 1960s, when synthetic materials first found widespread usage in boat interiors as a cost-saving device, boats soon looked worse than the inside of a trailer home. Cheap carpeting covered floors, walls, and ceiling. Curtains that looked like dishtowels adorned every window. Artificial woodwork, soon to delaminate, trimmed bulkheads covered with padded textured vinyl fabrics.

Today the trend has gone from trailer to Trump, and every boat, large or small, must look like the inside of an Atlantic City casino or an upscale shopping mall.

Sociologists and economists are stumbling over themselves in their eagerness to tell us that the post-war years have created a heightening of expectation in America unlike anything in history. They tell us that the idealism of the sixties and the relative asceticism of the oil crisis era were gleefully and gratefully abandoned during the 1980s in a long-repressed orgy of self-gratifying consumerism freed by easy credit and perceived prosperity. It is no coincidence, then, that pleasure boating more than doubled in size during the 1980s. Average boat horsepower skyrocketed, and so did the level of luxury expected in the smallest of boats. Parallel demands for excessive power and excessive luxury have been prime driving forces behind boat development since the die was cast after World War II.

The New Rumrunners

And now there is something different, a more sinister form of consumerism that has made its influence felt on the benign science of pleasure boat design.

On February 3, 1987, successful boatbuilder and former powerboat racer Don Aronow was publicly executed, gang-style, "in a hail of .45 caliber gunfire," as he sat in his Mercedes-Benz on "Thunderboat Row," Miami's 188th Street.* Suddenly the world became aware that the days of the rumrunner had returned, and that speedboat builders, as in the 1920s, had been making deals with the devil.

In the early days of prohibition, tramp freighters had been able to take on legal cargoes of liquor at Canadian, Bermudan, Bahamian, and Cuban ports, drop anchor outside the three-mile limit near American cities, and wait for their customers to come to them. Soon over 150 ships were lined up off the east coast between Atlantic City and Montauk. The prohibition authorities were helpless for a time, since they had neither boats nor budgetary allotments for boats. When the government extended the definition of "International Waters" to twelve miles, and spent some money to equip its agents with suitable watercraft, boat speed became a precious commodity.

The exploits of rumrunners like Bill McCoy, who was known for integrity and quality and has lent his name to our vernacular in the saying "the real McCoy," and their

* Anonymous, 1991.

boats, such as *Cigarette*, fascinated the American public. *Cigarette* was a Liberty-engined commuter that had been built for a wealthy man, and then sold into service as a rum-runner. Capable of 45 knots, she evaded capture for many months until she tried to ram a police boat. Confiscated by the police, she was soon freed by the efforts of her owners' lawyers, and was back in service. Captured again, she became CG-911, and was used to chase and apprehend other rum-runners.

Ironically, the boats that put Aronow on the map half a century later were named *Cigarette* also. While there was very little outward similarity between Aronow's bright, sleek, and glamorous muscle boats and the doughty hodgepodge of rumrunners from yesteryear, there was a distinct parallel in purpose. Aronow's boats became the conveyance of choice for nighttime meetings with offshore vessels as during the '20s, but this time the cargo was different: cocaine.

Aronow, like many boatbuilders in the '20s, had soon developed a mixed clientele of smugglers and law enforcement agencies, each hell-bent on outperforming the other, and lives hung in the balance. Aronow's life became one of them. The tension that resulted from such opposing needs had created a new breed of boat, putting speeds over 90 miles per hour into the hands of the casual boat buyer.

Today, *Cigarette* has become a generic term like "rum-runner," referring to any brand of long, muscular, open runabout, linked, often stereotypically, to evocations of conspicuous masculine virility. Cigarette's own advertisements feature a couple who have obviously just finished having sex together, and the caption (she is speaking) says, "Does this mean I can have a ride in your Cigarette?" With this blatant promise of sexual gratification and evocation of predatory sex appeal, it is hardly surprising that sales of most "Cigarette" boats have held up well during the recent recession. Why?

Commodity businesses are known to do well during hard

times, and the implicit guarantee of sex as a marine recreational product is as close to a true commodity as pleasure boating has ever come. Builders of smaller powerboats have, of course, tried persistently to infuse their humbler craft with the mythos of the muscle boats, with limited success.

The University of Wisconsin study of boating duty cycles* revealed that an average boater spends only 4.9 percent of his time in the 90–100 percent engine rpm range, and 10.4 percent of his time in the 80–90 percent engine rpm range. The busiest engine rpm category was, in fact, the 0–10 percent range, dead slow, occupying 17.1 percent of a boater's time on the water.

So if only 5 or 10 percent of a boater's time is spent in the upper speed ranges, and over 30 percent at subplaning speeds, a question is raised: why is the boating industry selling raw speed, and all the excess baggage that goes with it?

The answer is, of course, that the almost universally male boat buyer just likes to know that the speed and power are there. The history and mythology of powerboating have convinced him he must have it.

And from this we are hard pressed to avoid the conclusion that as much as 420 million gallons of oil and poisonous hydrocarbons are being spilled into our waterways and breathing air each year because people are carrying around enormous amounts of unused horsepower—operating their engines and powertrains, set up to achieve peak efficiency at top engine rpm's, in their most inefficient speed ranges.

And they are carrying it simply because they *like to have it there.*

But what are the alternatives?

* Morgan and Lincoln, 1989.

4

Good Energy

Establishing the Criteria

THERE ARE THREE DISTINCT constituent elements to consider if pleasure boating is going to initiate modifications that will prevent more than 400 million gallons of hydrocarbon material from entering our air and water every year. They are, first, the *fuels* or other energy sources that will provide the cleanest energy; second, the most efficient type of *propulsion*; and third, how the *shape* of the boat itself affects efficiency. Criteria and specifications must be established.

First, *energy*. Sources of energy should be renewable to the greatest possible degree, nontoxic in composition and in post-combustion by-product, safe, readily adaptable to existing distribution infrastructures, and cost-competitive. Ideally, they must also be produced by low-effort processes geographically near the end user to minimize detrimental corollary effects, such as geopolitical instability and pollution from ocean spills or road transport. Every aspect of a fuel's impact upon society and the environment, from cradle to grave, must be taken into consideration. There must be recognition of the imperfect fuels that are available today, and of more perfect fuels that are coming, but will be in limited supply for the near-term.

Second, *propulsion.* Propulsion systems must be selected or developed for greatest efficiency, lowest possible emissions, adaptability to the best fuels, lowest unit cost, and greatest reliability. Corollary pollution, from manufacturing and transportation, must also be taken into consideration. We must select the options that are practical today, and focus on choices we will be able to make in a few years.

Third, *boats* themselves must be designed to make the most of gains in fuel and motor application. They should be inexpensive to build and easy to maintain. Resistance characteristics, which in all cases should be low, must match the power, fuel consumption, and emissions profiles of the installed engines. The energy, engine, and boat must all be mutually compatible. It would be futile, for instance, to outfit a deep-V offshore muscle boat with tiny electric motors and heavy lead-acid batteries. The deep-V has very high resistance characteristics at low speeds, and would drain the best battery bank within a disappointingly short time. Equally futile would be the installation of a powerful clean-burning high-efficiency internal combustion (IC) engine, with all its exhaust catalysts and regeneration systems, in a displacement hull. Easily driven by teaspoons of energy at low speeds, the displacement hull stubbornly absorbs all the energy that can be put into it after it has reached a certain speed $(V = 1.34\sqrt{\text{LWL}})$,* and refuses to give up another tenth of a knot. Similarly, it would make little sense to outfit a long-distance cruiser with electric motors and lead-acid batteries, but such a setup could work very nicely for a local water taxi service.

Good motors and good boats will be the subjects of fol-

---

* That velocity (V) is generally about 1.34 times the square root of its load waterline length (LWL).

lowing chapters. Here we must first look at the confusing array of fuels which will power the coming generations of integrated marine propulsion systems.

The Rule of Capture

The development of internal combustion engines and the attitudes that have caused uncontrollable proliferation of tail-pipe hydrocarbon emissions have been driven, to a great degree, by the character of the petroleum industry.

In the summer of 1856, Samuel Kier was a very unhappy man. He owned a number of salt springs in the Allegheny Mountains of Pennsylvania, and had been drilling artesian wells to bring the healthful waters to the surface for bottling and sale on the brisk patent medicine market. Unfortunately, most of his new wells had been spoiled by a mysterious and rare substance called petroleum. Soon, however, after learning that petroleum had been flowing in nearby streams for as long as anyone could remember, and that the local Indian population considered it to be a potent medicine, Kier decided to make the best of things and bottle it. Thus was born Kier's Petroleum, a sure cure for cholera, consumption, bronchitis, and diseases of the liver. The dose was three teaspoons three times daily. By that winter, sales were booming.

Then, in 1858, a man named Edward Drake, an ex–railroad conductor and ersatz colonel who had been thinking long and hard about ways to extract petroleum from the ground, saw a bottle of Kier's in a New York shop window. On the label was a picture of an artesian well derrick, and it got him thinking: why wouldn't a water well work as an oil well? Armed with that inspirational image, he raised the money to drill a test hole in the same Allegheny hills, and on August 23, 1859, at a depth of 69.5 feet, he struck oil. It was soon flowing at a rate of 25 barrels a day.

But who was buying oil? Cars, trucks, power plants, and plastics were unknown. The internal combustion engine had yet to be successfully developed. Only a German, Marcus, and a Frenchman, Lenoir, were tinkering with engines, and they were Europeans, experimenting in noble obscurity. There was, however, a widespread need for low-cost lamp oil to light millions of households and lubricate the machines of growing industries around the world. Unlike whale oil or a number of vegetable derivatives that were in use, production costs of petroleum were essentially nil. It just flowed out of the ground.

By November 1861 the first export barrels of Pennsylvania crude oil were loaded onto the sailing brig *Elizabeth Watts*, bound for England. The shipping rate was $1 per barrel. The captain could not find a good crew to work on deck above a cargo of oil, however, and had to secure a crew by plying men with liquor in the numerous Philadelphia waterfront saloons. The *Elizabeth Watts* sailed a crooked course down the Delaware the following day, but arrived in London without mishap.

Soon many sailing ships were outfitted with iron tanks for bulk shipment of oil, but steamship companies were very reluctant to enter the trade. In 1864 sailing ships carried 32 million gallons of Pennsylvania crude over the world's oceans, and it wasn't until 1879 that the first steamer was converted for carrying oil. Several sailing oil tankers were lost at sea with their cargoes, and one surviving captain reported that "the oil seemed to move faster than the water, and in rough weather, when the vessel pitched forward, the oil would rush down and force the vessel into the waves."* Evidently, tank baffles had not yet been developed. By 1885, over 1,000 vessels were carrying oil in bulk.

The first oil pipelines, 6 inches in diameter, were built in

---

* Clark, 1958.

1865. A barrel of oil cost $1.25 to ship by rail, but only 17¢ by pipeline.

From humble beginnings in 1870, John D. Rockefeller's Standard Oil, and its many proliferating subsidiaries, in twelve short years gained control over 90 percent of the shipping, refining, and marketing of petroleum products. With absolute control of the infrastructure, Rockefeller then had an easy time dominating the production sector as well, and by 1913 Standard Oil was absolute master of the American petroleum industry.

Rumors of mysterious disappearances and scandals surrounding bribed congressmen brought the Rockefellers under increasingly intense government scrutiny. Smaller producers had been fighting bitterly against Standard Oil's strong-arm tactics, and as early as 1876 they had already hauled the Rockefellers before the Supreme Court. The earliest antitrust laws were written specifically against Standard Oil's excesses, but were to provide no protection whatsoever against similar strategies pursued by a foreign company on U.S. soil.

Frenchman Henri Deterding's Royal Dutch Shell corporation, based in London, exploited this weakness and entered the American market in a manner more rapacious than the Rockefellers could have dreamed. Although Josephus Daniels, Secretary of the Navy, pleaded before Congress in 1919 for the nationalization of oil to protect America's future interests, free-market forces defeated the measure. Deterding kept his subsidiaries legally separate, and so was untouchable. Shell opened huge fields in California and Oklahoma, and in one year, from 1921 to 1922, U.S. oil "production" jumped from 9 billion barrels to 19 billion barrels.

Standard Oil, although hobbled by one-sided regulations, countered Shell's moves as vigorously as possible, and the two giants, often in company with many smaller companies as well, clustered above underground pools of oil, milking their competing leases for every penny they could yield. Wells were drilled by the hundreds, shoulder to shoulder, over the same fast-dwindling pools of oil.

The very thought that Deterding was legally stealing oil that should rightfully have been Standard Oil's would spur Rockefeller to sink ever more wells and pump ever harder. Deterding would then counter with still more wells and intensified pumping himself, followed by all the minor companies, and thus the entire oil industry became obsessed with a single dominant object: to suck every last drop out of the ground faster than the other guy, and devil take the hindmost. That self-perpetuating cycle of belligerent schoolyard territorialism was called the Rule of Capture, and masquerading as sound free-market business, it led to such furious rates of "production" that the United States was providing 70 percent of the world's oil during the 1920s.

Calls for conservation were laughed at, much as they are today, even though America was known to have relatively modest, finite oil reserves. Confusion reigned in Congress as partisan politics and the abstruse pragmatics of the free-market system prevented government from taking any positive action.

With drilling and pumping fired by a desperate need to one-up the competition, "production" far outstripped storage and shipping capacity even before Deterding's time. Pipelines and rail systems, operating at capacity, couldn't handle the burgeoning flow. Unshippable oil had to be stored first in huge wooden cisterns, then in earthen ponds, then dammed lake reservoirs, all of which were soon full, and finally the flood of surplus "production" had to run, uncontrolled, into streambeds and farmlands. Oil in storage ponds soon evaporated, leaving thick residues which were removed periodically—by burning. An agency commissioner named

Sells was supplied figures which proudly showed that one California tract he visited was "producing" 40,000 barrels of oil per day, but he noted that its pipelines could carry away only 8,000 barrels. Oilfield operators estimated their losses from seepage and evaporation to be 50 percent of the total "production," and one east Texas observer stated, "There is more oil flowing daily down the Bayou in this field, and the Tiger creek in the Cushing field, than is produced in the entirety of many well-known fields."*

Natural gas could not yet be marketed, so gas wellheads were left wide open to blow unrestricted into the atmosphere, losing 30 million, 40 million, and 50 million cubic feet per day, for weeks and months at a time. Hundreds of billions of cubic feet were released during the period from 1910 to 1915. In January of 1914, one particularly strong gas well ran amok at Healdton, Oklahoma. Visitors to the site were flagged down and warned not to smoke or drive their automobiles for fear of setting off an apocalyptic explosion. Teams of horses towed cars and trucks through the field to lessen the probability of igniting the gas. One Louisiana well contractor, unable to light the boiler in the steam engine powering his drill rig and losing money every day, tapped a well and ran his engine on pure pressurized natural gas. Air at many oilfields was thick with the blue haze of natural gas, and miles away the gas could be clearly seen accumulating in low-lying wooded areas.

The ground was saturated with oil. Cars and trucks entering the oilfields would soon bog down to their axles in tarry pools of it. Heavy rains often washed out the earthen reservoirs, allowing oil to flood over miles of farmland. Lightning strikes would start fires, and one month-long fire at an Oklahoma field destroyed a 40-million-cubic-foot gas well, two flowing oil wells, six 55,000-barrel steel tanks,

---

* Clark, 1958.

several wooden ones, and many ponds of oil. Thousands of ducks and geese, attracted by the shimmering ponds, were trapped in them forever. Volunteer bird shampooing was a human impulse unknown at the time.

Despite the fact that most of that wasted "production" should have stayed in the ground until needed, and despite the efforts of many farsighted individuals, the Rule of Capture remained the dominant law of the oil industry. Conservation began to take hold during the isolationist years of the late 1930s, but the advent of World War II once again mandated a return to maximum profligacy.

Such is the background of the oil industry, which has guided our domestic and international politics, sent millions of men to war, and remains to this day—like the pleasure boating industry—congenitally opposed to conservation and environmental quality.

Energy sources presently available for consideration are gasoline, diesel fuel, alcohol fuels like ethanol and methanol, natural gas, hydrogen, stored electricity from batteries, and on-board production of electricity via fuel cells.

All the liquid fuels, whether petroleum-derived, like gasoline, diesel, and natural gas, or biomass-derived, like ethanol and methanol, are hydrocarbons. They possess as their primary physical characteristics an array of hydrogen atoms linked to carbon atoms. Whether as simple as acetylene (CH_2), or formed of dazzlingly complex molecular arrays, the central chemical theme of liquid fuels is the alliance of hydrogen and carbon. Other ingredients are added to benefit combustion characteristics, which in turn relate to the refinement and improvement of efficiency and emissions.

Gasoline

Common gasoline is not the simple thing we think it to be. It was discovered by accident as a by-product of a process called "cracking." Prior to 1860 crude oil had been refined by heating in huge cauldrons, a slow and costly procedure. One day in that year, however, a refining engineer had to take an unauthorized absence from his post to respond to family problems, so he arranged his ventilation system to increase atmospheric pressure in the room, thus prolonging the burn time of his fires. When he returned, he found that the increased heat and pressure had created a much clearer product than before, and something new: gasoline. The engineer was reprimanded, however, and it wasn't until 1910 that a patent was issued to protect cracking.* During the interim some refineries tried to burn gasoline as fuel, but it was dangerous, and there was no real market for it, so most just let it run off into sewers.

Early forms of gasoline were simple, and burned cleanly. Today, however, it is a complex blend that varies from manufacturer to manufacturer, from grade to grade, and even by location and season. Gasoline combustion emissions contain zinc, platinum, rhodium, cadmium, and iron plus six fundamental hydrocarbons, eleven basic polycyclic hydrocarbons, cyanides, ammonia, nitrous oxides, hydrogen sulfide, sulfur dioxide, ten individual aldehydes and ketones, phenols, amines, nitrosamines, and myriad variants.

Pressured by politicians and the EPA, the oil industry typically responds with new, even more complex formulations. Unfortunately, like a boat racing rule, these formulations target the letter of the law, not the spirit, and in the course of reducing one substance may well increase several others, or add some new ones.

---

* Hanighen, 1934.

For example: the Colorado oxygenated fuels program. The city of Denver, Colorado, experiences a carbon monoxide crisis every winter.* The combined effects of cold weather and high altitude cause automobiles to emit excessive amounts of carbon monoxide. Temperature inversions often develop, trapping the carbon monoxide, which builds to unhealthy concentrations. Since the winter of 1987–1988, Colorado has been making oxygenated gasoline available at pumps in several key areas. Extra oxygen molecules from additives in the gasoline attach to the carbon monoxide (CO) to form carbon dioxide (CO_2). This has reduced the local crisis, but carbon dioxide is still a major greenhouse gas. Also, although oxygenated fuel promotes a leaner burn in automobile engines, without precise monitoring of individual equivalence (rich / lean) ratios, the lean burn may very well produce greater emissions of nitrogen oxides, a key component of the smog reaction,† although I have been emphatically assured by representatives of the EPA that *"oxygenated fuels reduce tail-pipe emissions."* Thus, like the Argonauts fighting warriors springing up from sown dragon's teeth, we sometimes find ourselves slaying one enemy only to have two take its place.

Gasoline, if handled with care throughout its life in the procurement, refinement, and combustion phases, can be a magnificent fuel. It is inexpensive to produce and contains 50 times more energy by weight than lead-acid batteries. The advent of catalytic converters and a host of sophisticated engine refinements have combined to reduce gasoline-burning engine emissions to single-digit percentages of what they were only twenty years ago.

Federal law is mandating a further lowering of nationwide automotive hydrocarbon emission levels, to 0.25 gram per mile. California is moving toward 0.04 gram per mile,

---

* Gallagher et al., 1990.
† Dempster and Shore, 1990.

a step that will be copied by the other states adopting California's guidelines. Nobody is quite sure how, precisely, these goals will be met, but the process will involve fuel technology in concert with motor engineering refinements, low-resistance automobile bodies, and improved emission-control devices like catalytic converters. Cleaning up the pleasure boat problem will involve the same combination of factors.

We have been hearing about high-tech "reformulated" gasoline in recent years. Gulf Advent 21, Shell SU2000E, and Arco EC-1 are examples of this trend, promising higher octane, cleaner engines, and lower emissions.* These claims result from component shuffling and additive inclusion. Ingredients of gasoline, such as low-octane naphtha, are removed during the refining process, reformed into a material that better meets the new criteria, and then reintroduced. Additives for oxygenation and detergency are simply concocted and poured into the fuel. Sometimes undesirable components, such as butane and benzene, are chemically removed or reduced.

Boating associations and engine manufacturers contend that "modern gasoline formulations" clog outboard motors with excessive carbon deposits, causing damage to the engines. This has in turn spawned another generation of additives, with unknown formulations and unknown results, for *re*-reformulation of the gasoline. It seems highly unlikely that the added oxygen from oxygenated fuels would cause poor and uneven combustion, as claimed. To the contrary. But boaters are not the only people who are suspicious of change.

According to the *New York Post*,† service stations in New York City have been ordered to convert to reformulated gasoline to meet air pollution standards set by the federal

---

* Skorupa, 1991.
† Steier, 1991.

Clean Air Act. The 1,000 gasoline dealers in New York City are outraged at having to sell fuel costing an additional 4¢ per gallon (although gasoline in Europe costs much, much more than in the United States). They are outraged—even though tests at a Brooklyn laboratory showed the new fuels cutting carbon monoxide by 15 percent and hydrocarbons by 10 percent. The city's own municipal fleet operators have resisted the oxygenated fuel because they claim that they are being charged an additional 18¢ per gallon at the wholesale level. This may, of course, be nothing more than political posturing.

Alcohol Fuels from Biomass

While millions of dollars are being spent on the development of so-called clean gasolines, many people believe that the alcohol fuels, ethanol and methanol, served up straight or in a cocktail with gasoline, may be the answer to reducing nationwide fleet emissions with the added benefit of eliminating our dependency on imported oil. Emission tests seem to support the notion that alcohols burn cleaner,[*] reducing hydrocarbon emissions by half in uncatalyzed engines, and somewhat less dramatically in a variety of catalyzed configurations. In addition, methanol has been used successfully for almost 400,000 miles in buses outfitted with diesel engines.[†] Detroit Diesel Corporation's methanol-fueled compression-ignition engine model 6V-92 is on track to become the new standard for the urban transit industry, replacing the older 6V-92 diesel engines.[‡] Because methanol also burns well in spark-ignition engines, this presents the tantalizing possibility of a monofuel transportation system.

[*] Santoro et al., 1990.
[†] Eberhard et al., 1990.
[‡] Miller, 1992.

Alcohol fuels are made by distillation of biomass materials. Most plants are able to yield fuel through a variety of fermentation processes, but some are more practical than others. Ethanol, also known as grain alcohol, can be made from corn, wheat, rice, oats, rye, beets, sugarcane, and other common crops. If, for example, 40 percent of the American corn crop were diverted to fuel production, we could end our importation of foreign oil and, in fact, become energy exporters again. Another very intriguing thought. Unfortunately, most biomass distillation is not yet economically feasible (based on correct U.S. gasoline prices) in our markets, and the modest levels that presently exist continue to depend on government subsidies. The nation of Brazil, by contrast, depends greatly on biomass fuels, deriving as much as 50 percent of its energy needs from waste sugarcane.

In its most basic form, methanol, also known as wood alcohol, is three parts hydrogen, one part oxygen, and one part carbon, although in all probability it, along with ethanol, will be modified extensively to improve burn and further reduce emissions. Methanol is made primarily from coal, natural gas, and a variety of woods and wood by-products or effluent.

Both methanol and ethanol have higher octane ratings than gasoline. Methanol has been used by racecar drivers for decades. Even so, these materials are less energy-dense than gasoline: a gallon of ethanol contains only as much energy as two-thirds of a gallon of gasoline.*

Today alcohol fuels are being used as additives in 10 percent solution with gasoline, sold as super unleaded, through several states in the corn belt, Massachusetts, and New York.†
The Alternative Motor Fuels Act of 1988 is supposed to prod America toward widespread use of alcohol and natural gas

* Reece, 1991.
† Miller, 1992.

fuels by improving their competitive position in relation to conventional gasoline and diesel fuel.

From my viewpoint, if the act has had any success it is one of the best-kept secrets in our country. According to President Bush's "national energy strategy," there will be 80 million dual-fuel vehicles in operation by the year 2005. But I have not yet been able to fill my tank with any form of alternative fuel, in any of my travels.

Biomass fuels, although emitting fewer greenhouse gases, generate large quantities of post-combustion formaldehyde, which is not a suitable replacement for the emissions from gasoline. Seventeen different new catalysts, however, have been recently tested in spark-ignition engines, and three of them were capable of reducing formaldehyde emissions by over 98 percent, well into the acceptable range.* Under compression ignition, methanol produces much less formaldehyde.

Corn ethanol, in quantities over 800 million gallons per year, is in about 8 percent of the nation's vehicle fuels. The Corn Board tells us that just 40 percent of America's abundant corn crop would power all our energy needs. Unfortunately, corn is a fairly demanding crop, requiring lots of water and prime farmland, and with today's technology it takes the energy contained in 12 gallons of corn ethanol to make 10 gallons (like the American penny, which costs 3¢ to make). Federal incentives of approximately 60¢ per gallon, procured through the efforts of a powerful farm lobby, subsidize the production of corn ethanol.

Ethanol produced from nonfood crops, such as short-rotation drought-resistant hardwood trees, grasses, and legumes, will be widely available at competitive pricing by the year 2000, and probably sooner in many areas. The U.S. Department of Energy is investing $72 million in a five-year program to achieve that goal. Made by a process

* Santoro et al., 1990.

involving enzymation, hydrolysis, and fermentation, non-food ethanol is expected to cost only 60¢ per gallon without subsidies. Lower-quality land can be planted with profit-able crops, and if, as the Department of Agriculture main-tains, 200 million acres (25 percent of present space occupied by operating farms and commercial forests) can be con-verted to fuel crops, we can replace more than half of the fossil fuels now used for transportation.* Once again, we can see alluring images of independence from the intran-sigent Middle Eastern oil potentates, the creation of mil-lions of jobs, positive trade balances, and shrinking deficits.

Nonfood ethanol is widely regarded to be a potentially near-perfect fuel. It is made from renewable materials and does not deplete scarce resources. The emissions from its combustion are much more manageable than those from fossil fuels. Most intriguing, however, is the fact that *the plants which are grown to make ethanol consume as much carbon dioxide in photosynthesis as the fuel ethanol will pro-duce in combustion.* Such an elegant balance is the essence of ecology. All we need to do, after all, is imitate nature.

A particular benefit to using alcohol fuels in the marine market is their tolerance to water contamination. In tests with a diesel engine fueled by methanol containing 2 per-cent water, not only were some areas of combustion actually improved, but some emissions were lower as well.

One caveat: a nation moving toward general use of bio-mass fuels will have to watch corollary effects very closely. In Brazil, where 44 million cars are fueled with sugarcane ethanol, the discharge of untreated ethanol by-products has fouled many of the rivers in that country's northwestern regions.† Hazards exist from overexuberant agricultural trends as well. History is littered with the ruins of civiliza-tions that mismanaged their precious resources of water and

---

* Goodman and Cook, 1991.
† Barber, 1991.

fertile ground, and the lessons of history often have to be painfully relearned.*

Alcohol fuels are dangerous to handle, requiring more sophisticated distribution hardware, and being corrosive, cannot be stored in the conventional steel fuel tanks most cars and trucks are equipped with. Because of these limitations, and problems of availability, alcohol fuels and most other potential alternate fuels are being tested primarily in municipal, county, state, federal, and corporate fleets.

Diesel Fuel

Diesel fuel is being targeted for reformulation in a manner similar to gasoline, but it is already a better source of energy than gasoline. Diesel in usable form virtually pours out of a spigot two-thirds of the way up a refinery's fractionating tower, unlike gasoline which in its most basic applications must undergo cracking and blending with naphtha and many other dubious chemical additives. Diesel fuel (in diesel engines) produces more foot-pounds of torque per gallon and per mile than gasoline, at a lower cost.

But emission standards for diesel engines will be very difficult to comply with. By 1991, urban buses were supposed to have met a standard of 0.1 gram of particulate emission (which we see as smoke) per horsepower-hour. They did not. By 1994 particulates are to be much, much lower still. A bus developing between 20 (idling) and 200 (accelerating) horsepower on a constant cycle of stop-and-go driving (the very worst from an emissions-control standpoint) will be allowed about 5 grams per hour, or about a quarter of a gram per mile, depending on traffic conditions. Even though this figure is roughly comparable, on a per-horsepower basis, to allowable emissions from a passenger car's gasoline

* Reisner, 1987; Ponting, 1990.

engine, the cost/benefit ratio is far superior because buses carry many passengers versus one or two in an average automobile, and trucks carry tons of cargo.

Despite the obvious particulate smoke associated with diesel engines, their overall hydrocarbon output is much less than that from gasoline engines. The Achilles' heel of the diesel is its prolific output of NOx—oxides of nitrogen—which, with hydrocarbons, form smog.

Most of the advances in clean diesel applications are coming from internal power-plant engineering and pollution control appendages to engine systems. Additional benefits will arise from reformulation of diesel fuel, which has a characteristically high sulfur dioxide emission content, high aromatic hydrocarbon content, and low cetane (a hydrocarbon of the methane family that helps ignition). Reformulated diesel fuel will have reduced sulfur and aromatics content, and will contain cetane-enhancing additives.

Natural Gas

Compressed natural gas, or CNG, has many attractive features. High in methane, it is a naturally occurring petroleum product found in significant quantities in North America. It is now being found as deep as 30,000 feet below ground, and a new theory among geologists holds that natural gas may not be fossil-derived at all, but may be formed in seepage pockets from pressures at the earth's core. A number of sources report that the United States could become completely energy independent (for a finite period of time) once again if it converted entirely to the use of natural gas.[*]

CNG requires almost nothing in the way of refinement—occasional sulfur and moisture contaminants have to be removed—but delivery and storage add to costs because the

[*] Miller, 1992.

gas must be maintained under pressure, sometimes as a cryogenic liquid (LNG). Even so, it costs less than gasoline per unit of energy. In upstate New York, the CNG equivalent of one gallon of gasoline costs about 85¢ in winter, when demand is high, and about 50¢ in summer. The United States already has the best-developed system of natural gas distribution in the world,* but very little of it is currently accessible in filling-station format, and obstacles to pipeline routing and construction are likely to delay further CNG distribution. Natural gas does reduce the power output of converted engines by 3 to 5 percent, despite its 130-octane rating, and requires the installation of strong fuel tanks capable of withstanding the high pressures of CNG.

Emissions from combustion of CNG are generally much lower than those from gasoline, diesel fuel, and even the alcohol fuels. There are no particulates, and engine residue deposits are virtually nonexistent. One county official told me that in his fleet, "You can forget about having to change spark plugs." CNG is far safer than gasoline and propane, and because it evaporates instantly and is stored in bomb-proof three-quarter-inch-thick filament-wound fiberglass tanks, it may also be statistically safer than diesel fuel.

Engine conversion kits and fuel tanks are readily available, as are purpose-built engines, and arrangements for filling can be made with local fuel suppliers and utilities. These enticing characteristics prompted the western New York State communities of Buffalo and nearby Tonawanda to convert many of the vehicles in their municipal fleets to natural gas. Tonawanda's sewer cleaning truck had been diesel-powered, and had needed oil changes twice a week, but after the diesel was removed and a CNG engine installed, the first oil charge was still clean after six months of continuous operation. Samples were so clean that a Washington, D.C., laboratory returned them as untestable.

---

* Reece, 1991.

While most of these vehicles are able to change fuels at the flip of a switch, choosing between natural gas and gasoline and thereby depending less on limited CNG distribution, GM and Ford are now marketing dedicated CNG pickups and vans to municipalities in California. The mass transit systems of Toronto and Pittsburgh are already converted to natural gas, and test vehicles are scheduled to begin running in Syracuse, Rochester, Binghamton, and Nassau County, New York, during 1992. In Weston, Massachusetts, near Boston, the school district converted two school buses to run on natural gas. Art Wagman, a department employee charged with overseeing the test, stated that much less maintenance was required, and that the district expected to save 17 percent on fuel costs.* In all cases, fleet operators report similar satisfactory experiences with the CNG.

CNG is also a very promising source of derived fuel hydrogen—anticipated to cost less than one-third of hydrogen produced by other methods. It is also the most likely fuel to power a near-term generation of fuel cells. Some 500,000 natural gas–powered vehicles are already in worldwide use today, most of them in Europe and Canada.

It is worth noting that while unmodified diesel engines will not run well on CNG, there has been some progress in developing commercial CNG engines from diesels adapted to spark ignition. CNG storage may be too bulky for conversion of existing boats, but boats designed specifically for CNG fuel could be extremely viable. LNG, which is a liquid, would be more viable still. The problem, as with all alternative energies, is distribution.

Fuel Hydrogen

The best fuel of all, ironically, is the one with the fewest practical applications in service to date: hydrogen. Long-

* AP, 1991a.

term considerations point to hydrogen as the fuel of the future. It is the most plentiful element in the known universe, and rapid-oxidation by-products, such as those that characterize fuel cell operation, are nothing but small wisps of water vapor. Outright combustion adds a tiny amount of nitrogen oxides. And despite this wonderfully low emission profile, hydrogen is far more powerful, by weight, than gasoline.

The history of fuel-hydrogen development is remarkably colorful, dating back hundreds of years. Most of us would recognize it first, however, as the fuel powering Nemo's submarine *Nautilus* in the Jules Verne classic *Twenty Thousand Leagues Under the Sea.* The hydrogen in coal gas fueled many early engines, and during the worst days of England's isolation in 1939 and 1940, enormous flimsy bags were fitted to the roofs of cars and filled with coal gas for fuel, replacing scarce or nonexistent gasoline.

In 1942, U.S. vice-president Henry Wallace witnessed a demonstration of an automobile engine that ran very successfully on hydrogen. The system had been designed by an unknown Bolivian named Francisco Pacheco.* Through a simple process involving aluminum and magnesium immersed in salt water, Pacheco was producing workable quantities of highly flammable hydrogen. Wallace encouraged him to bring his invention to the United States, but after years and years of struggle and demonstrations, working as an oil burner repairman to feed his family, Pacheco is still unknown, and although he is the possessor of many key patents, his process lies fallow. On July 17, 1974, he ran a 26-foot boat for nine hours using the electrochemical reaction between magnesium and aluminum in seawater for fuel energy.

Two other lonely individuals who have done extensive but

* Westdyk, 1989.

unrewarded work with fuel hydrogen are Stan Meyer and John Lorenzen. Meyer is a combative technocentric who concentrates much of his energy toward obtaining a profusion of patents for such arcane gadgets as a Hydrogen Gas Injector System, Electrical Pulse Generator, Gas Generator Voltage Control Circuit, and Resonant Cavity Hydrogen Generator, along with processes such as a Controlled Hydrogen Gas Flame, and a Start-Up / Shut-Down for a Hydrogen Gas Burner. Flush from the proven success of his water-fuel–powered, VW-engined dune buggy, he now plans to win the Indianapolis 500 in a hydrogen-powered racecar. His news releases are four-page chronicles of his battle with the Establishment, and carry the message "Water Fuel Cell, Job 38 22–23, Jesus Christ is Lord."*

John Lorenzen is very different. He hasn't the time of day for hyperbole, and yet Roger Smith, then chairman of GM, and Henry Ford II have both made pilgrimages to his central Iowa farm, along with hundreds of other energy aficionados. Lorenzen is indeed the stuff of which legends are made, fulfilling the best tradition of the understated, rough-edged American barnyard tinkerer.

In the 1930s, when the Rural Electrification Administration people came to his door, Lorenzen said, "No thanks. Don't know what I'd do with any more electricity." Powered by two windmills (with a third on standby) and an array of reclaimed storage batteries, some of them Edison units over forty years old, Lorenzen has had all the power he and his wife could use, and never did hook up to a utility line. When he added a solar heating system, also made from everyday scrap, Lorenzen realized he had some extra energy and set to work to produce hydrogen. After a number of trial-and-error experiments—one of which blew a regulator off his storage bottle—he achieved some significant break-

---

* Thompson, 1988–1989.

throughs, elegant in their simplicity, all made from surplus and scrap.*

But the innovation that has attracted most attention is in his old Ford pickup. Lorenzen takes a few stray amps from his engine's alternator, which, like most vehicle charging systems, is loafing much of the time, and runs the power to electrodes immersed in a small plastic tank of water under the hood—a reclaimed windshield washer fluid tank. The electrical field between electrodes breaks the hydrogen–oxygen bond, releasing the two as a highly flammable gas. That gas is pulled into the carburetor by the engine's natural intake vacuum and results in a doubling of Lorenzen's gas mileage.

To date, no one has attempted to capitalize on this dead-simple gadget. It is too simple, too grand, too successful, and therefore, despite what our eyes can see and our minds understand, the perception is that it cannot possibly be true.

While some people still remember the awful *Hindenburg* disaster, the real problem with hydrogen lies in economics. Lorenzen's hydrogen-additive device works only because the alternator current used to electrolyze water into gas is "free"; it is there for the taking. One could not, however, start a cottage industry in hydrogen cracking because the power needed to make the gas would be greater than the energy available from the hydrogen.

Many countries are trying valiantly to synthesize hydrogen from coal, natural gas, methane, and a variety of other potential sources. Automakers, particularly European and Japanese, are busily building and demonstrating hydrogen-fueled engines that will drive the cars of the future. Hydrogen fuel cells have been used by NASA in space for years, and researchers are modeling their viability in transit buses.

* *Mother Earth News*, 1980.

Even the old Stirling engine has been promoted as a hydrogen motor. The only thing missing is a cheap source of the fuel.

It is deceptively easy to make hydrogen. You can make it in the kitchen by dunking two electrodes into water, plugging them into a wall socket, and collecting the result. I have done it. Or you can pour half an inch of muriatic acid (a commercial form of hydrochloric acid) into the bottom of a beer bottle, immerse the bottle in a pan of cooling water, and drop in a few small clippings of aluminum wire, and hydrogen will be produced in abundance. Place a balloon over the mouth of the bottle, and it will be collected. Tie off the balloon, ignite it with a cigarette lighter held at the end of a broomstick, and for an instant you will see the sun in miniature. *This is in no way a suggestion or recommendation that anyone try these experiments without proper supervision. Explosion and physical harm may result.*

The best chance for viable fuel hydrogen production, despite many complicated chemical processes that are being examined, bears a certain similarity to the underlying concomitant of Lorenzen's alternator-powered mileage enhancer: an energy source that is available, unused, and unclaimed.*

Such a source exists. Solar energy meets the criteria perfectly. Roughly 1,000 watts of energy falls upon every sunlit square yard of this planet. Most of it goes to work making wind and weather, and some "fuels" plants and animals—in fact, it was solar energy that created the vast pools of smelly black petroleum over the rights to which we are busily killing one another. It could even be said that we are already, technically, living in a solar economy. And always have been.

* Miller, 1992.

Solar:
The Ultimate Clean Energy

According to Joan Ogden of the Princeton University Center for Energy and Environmental Studies, it would take "only" 24,000 square miles of solar collectors, one-half of 1 percent of U.S. land area, to replace all the oil used in America.* There are two applicable techniques for adapting solar energy to hydrogen production: electricity produced by photovoltaics will slowly make hydrogen from water, and intense heat from sophisticated reflectors will break it out.† At a cost of, say, $5 million per square mile, using current polycrystalline silicon panel technology and giving a generous allowance for volume pricing to work its magic, the cost of such a job would be a staggering $5 trillion.

At first glance this is cost-prohibitive, to be sure, but since solar panels have a long established history of being glitch-proof and maintenance-free, a simple business amortization schedule tells a different story: over a twenty-year life span (in all likelihood much longer) the annual cost is broken down to $250 billion. Gone are the corollary or social costs of oil consumption, the damage to human beings, forests, lakes, rivers, buildings, and the atmosphere. Gone is one major aggravator of world political tensions, and gone are the costs of maintaining a shaky global balance of power. We're wasting more money than that already. It would be a bargain!

Solar energy itself can be stored by charging batteries with electrical current from panels, so the energy becomes readily accessible as, for instance, the motive force to drive a boat, or run its electrical systems. There are several differ

---

* Ogden cited in McDonnell, 1991.
† Dostrovsky, 1991.

ent kinds of "solar panels," all of them under the generic etymological umbrella of *photovoltaics.*

Amorphous silicon is the cheapest and, as one might expect, the least efficient, generally reaching peak efficiencies of 6 or 7 percent (capturing only 60 or 70 of those 1,000 watts per square yard). Amorphous panels are flexible and light in weight, but also break down within a few years from the effects of the sunlight they are built to capture.

Polycrystalline panels are also made of silicon, and are available in rigid, heavier formats. Peak efficiencies approach 10 percent, but the cost is doubled.

Single-crystal photovoltaics are the most efficient and, depending on the base material, can range in efficiency from silicon's 12 percent to near 30 percent from the toxic and very costly gallium arsenide crystal.

New forms of photovoltaics are under development by Westinghouse, Texas Instruments, and other corporations, but none approach the efficiency of single-crystal panels. Yet.*

Unlike most power technologies, which are rated by relatively conservative criteria, solar panels are rated for the amount of power they will capture at some mythical moment when they are perfectly aligned, the sun is high overhead, there are no clouds, fog, or smog, and Jupiter is in Orion. Many hours of watching the ammeter on my supposedly 10-amp panel set groaning along at 4 or 5 amps cured me of any plans I might have had for building a solar commuting car, solarizing my house, or any of a dozen other schemes I had been fervidly concocting. Even so, there is a strong potential for solar energy, in the right places, under the right circumstances. At best, however, solar panels are worth little in the world of transportation without the storage battery.

* Lewandowski, personal communication, 1990.

Ah, batteries. I think I hear Thomas Edison rolling over in his grave.

The Storage of Electricity

In 1899 a Belgian named Camille Jenatzy drove his electric car *Jamais Contente* ("never satisfied") to a world speed record by covering the flying kilometer at a fantastic speed of 65 miles per hour.* Distinguished scientists had been questioning, until that day, the human body's ability to withstand the stresses of speeds over a mile a minute. Photographs of the vehicle show it to be a double-ended riveted metal projectile on rubber tires, draped in its triumph with garlands of flowers and lovely maidens in diaphanous gowns: Jules Verne meets Maxfield Parrish.

The electric car remained a legitimate contender for the mantle of transport dominance well into Henry Ford's time. In 1902 Charles Baker, an American, was able to attain 85 miles per hour. Batteries did not give much range, true, but neither did they give noise, smoke, or endless mechanical failures, which were the concomitants of owning an "explosion-engine" car. Although internal combustion engines were gradually being silenced and made more reliable, many people, among them Thomas Alva Edison, felt strongly that the electric car was a much more civilized way to travel, range limitations notwithstanding.

Edison saw that the day of the horse was coming to an end, and that the future belonged to the motorized carriage.† Electricity looked like a good bet. In 1899, 90 percent of the motor cabs in downtown New York were electric. Carriage builders were producing electric cars by the hundreds, outfitting Studebaker and Columbia carriages with

* Mateucci, 1970.
† Josephson, 1959.

batteries and electric motors. Recent advances in the construction and capacity of lead-acid storage batteries had shown the way to what looked like the beginning of a long and highly productive series of technological developments. Edison felt comfortable approaching the science of storage batteries; after all, he had, through protracted and diligent effort, cracked the closely held secrets of the electric light, the phonograph, and motion pictures.

Edison, as always ahead of his time, also felt that the internal combustion engine had the capacity, if universally accepted, to infuse the entire world with choking smoke and shattering noise. Unfortunately, few shared his viewpoint.

Henry Ford, who was an employee of the Detroit Edison powerhouse, first met Thomas Edison at a conference in 1897, a meeting arranged by a mutual acquaintance named Dow. Dow had been after Ford, who was a good electrician, to forget the gas car he had been developing in his spare time and concentrate on an electric vehicle. The meeting was fateful because Ford, long an admirer of Edison's, received from the crusty older man his first real words of encouragement. After plying Ford with questions and listening to his thoughtful and intelligent answers, Edison banged his fist down on the table, saying, "Young man, that's the thing! You have it! Keep at it!"

Edison himself, meanwhile, had little on his mind but the "miniature reservoir of electric force." He said, "I don't think Nature would be so unkind as to withhold the secret of a good storage battery, if a real earnest hunt were made for it. I'm going to hunt."

. Unfortunately, ten years and countless thousands of experiments later, Nature was still withholding, and Edison's perfect battery was not yet. In the meantime, internal combustion technology had made great advances. A six-cylinder Rolls-Royce car had successfully completed a 10,000-mile endurance run, and Henry Ford had introduced the Model N, a precursor to his famous T, with a cheap and reliable 15-horsepower four-cylinder engine. The Model N cost only $600 and went 20 miles on a gallon of gasoline. The year was 1907.

Ford and Edison became lifelong friends, and eventually Edison did achieve something of a breakthrough in the storage battery with his alkaline-electrolyte nickel-flake-lithium-iron Edison Cell. By 1909, after testing the battery's metal casing by dropping prototypes repeatedly from the third story of his laboratory, Edison began production in earnest. The first year brought gratifying sales, totaling more than $1 million to delivery fleets, industry, power stations, mines, merchant and naval fleets, and makers of electric cars. Edison's batteries were lighter and stronger, low-maintenance, noncorrosive, and safe to use in the confined spaces of submarines and mines. They were much faster at recharging, dependable, and longer-lived than the older lead-acid types. Despite these advantages, and a long and profitable manufacturing history, Edison's nickel-iron battery was ultimately bypassed in favor of lead-acid and nickel-cadmium batteries because the Ni-Fe was slightly more costly, and therefore not so profitable, and because it couldn't deliver the powerful surges of amperage necessary to crank over a big diesel or a cold automobile engine.

For the next seventy years propulsion markets were owned, lock, stock, and barrel, by the interests of internal combustion engine manufacturing. Even at the beginning of the jet age, many IC engine makers, such as Rover, Rolls-Royce, and Hispano-Suiza, were among the first to build gas turbines.

In such a context, there was little incentive to improve the storage battery. It was perfectly adequate to operate starter motors and systems, augmented by a steady charge from engine-driven alternators. Corporate memory faded over the years, and by mid-century there were few engineers who could explain the fundamental theories of battery design. Factory hygiene also declined, and batteries are commonly built today with faulty cells and below-rating performance due to sloppy assembly and oxidation on the plates.

Batteries, and the few feeble attempts to base transportation upon their energy reserves, continued to disappoint innovators and the general public. As Edison himself said in the first decade of this century: "When a man gets on to accumulators [storage batteries] his inherent capacity for lying comes out."*

Worse, millions of tons of lead were randomly discarded and huge mounds of highly toxic cadmium manufacturing effluent were deposited and abandoned, leaving a bitter legacy for the inhabitants of many American communities.

But always there was a faint hope for the Great Battery Breakthrough. Every fifteen or twenty years a new generation of electrical engineers would become fascinated with the now-futuristic notion of clean, quiet transportation, and a new generation of tinkerers would try to pick up the faint traces of Edison's trail on the quest for the perfect electro-dynamic couple.

Rumors persist to this day that promising technologies have been bought by the oil companies from their eager and naive inventors for the express purpose of suppression deep in sub-basement vaults to prevent their emergence as a threat to the status quo of petrobusiness. A number of configurations that were very effective in laboratory conditions, such as sodium-sulfur, nickel-iron, nickel-zinc, and lithium ion, most of them known for over fifty years, remained paralyzed in a perpetual state of suspended development. In reality, there was no money to develop a finished product because there was no market for the finished product. And there was no market because there was no finished product.

Meanwhile, the worldwide proliferation of the internal combustion engine, driven by wars, burgeoning industry, international commerce, and the continued growth of a

* Clark, 1977.

widespread middle class, was indeed filling the air with choking smoke and shattering noise, exactly as Edison had foreseen. The highly visible and tangible deterioration of the human environment finally prompted citizens to force government, kicking and screaming, after decades of battle, to enact clean air legislation. The enforcement and fulfillment of that legislation have forced a nonspontaneous, but still very real, "market" for storage batteries upon the reluctant petroleum and internal combustion industries, thus breaking the chicken-or-egg deadlock.

Battery Development Today

Batteries store and then produce electricity through a flow of ions between a positive plate and a negative plate in a conductive medium called an electrolyte. Made of two different materials, these plates, or electrodes, produce what is called a "couple," a fortuitous molecular relationship that allows for a free and vigorous interchange of atomic particles. We all know of lead-acid, of course, but there are many more couples being actively examined for commercial use.

Some names you will be hearing in the future are:

> Lead-Acid: energy density (ED) 8–12 watt-hours
>   per pound of battery.
> Recirculating-Electrolyte Lead-Acid: ED 10–15.
> Recombinant Lead-Acid: ED 16.
> Composite Lead-Acid (Kevlar-cored lead grids):
>   ED 18–20.*
> Nickel-Iron: ED 20.
> Nickel-Zinc: ED 25–35.†
> Sodium-Sulfur: ED 50–200.

* Jay, personal communication, 1991.
† Reisner, personal communication, 1990.

Sulfur-Air: ED highly variable.
Iron-Air: ED highly variable.
Aluminum-Air: ED 170.
Zinc-Air: ED 90.
Nickel-Cadmium (NiCad): ED 8–12.
Silver-Zinc: ED 80.
High-Temperature Lithium Ion: ED 200.*
Sodium-Nickel-Chloride: ED 30–35.
Nickel Metal Hydride: ED 20–25.

Unfortunately we must not get too excited about all the terrific energy-density figures in this list. Virtually every new battery technology is haunted by what one MIT researcher calls a "show-stopper"—a problem that is stubbornly defying resolution. Nature still withholding its secrets. For example, of the most promising new couples, lithium is highly flammable and has to operate at 600 degrees, and sodium-sulfur, which is fantastically corrosive, must also remain molten at 300 degrees. Silver-zinc has been around for a long time and stores a great deal of energy, providing a tantalizing glimpse into the future of electric propulsion. It has been used successfully in demanding applications such as torpedoes, solar racecars, and Paul MacReady's record-holding *Solar Challenger.* But it is priced at ten times lead-acid on a cost per watt-hour basis, thirty or forty times lead-acid by weight. Then there is aluminum-air, which, while wonderfully energy-dense, can only produce current at a 20-amp rate, and so is incapable of surges of real power. It is being programmed for eventual application as a "range-extender" in electric vehicles,† to charge another set of batteries much as a generator would, and today exists in prototype form as a stationary generating medium.

Most of the new batteries are still confined to the lab,

* Thornton, personal communication, 1992.
† Lapp, personal communication, 1990.

with a host of logistical problems preventing practical field use. I heard a story about one prototype lithium ion battery that became so hot it caught fire and melted through a thick metal lab bench. Others are so complex they are not recognizable—more like machines than anything we normally think of as batteries. And some use such dangerous materials that manufacturing the batteries poses more environmental problems than their widespread use could solve.

Some really good, viable couples, however, like zinc-air, nickel-zinc, aluminum-air, and the exotic lead-acids, have gone through development and only await investment capital to begin production in earnest. Again, the chicken-and-egg situation is the problem; no money is available to develop the product because there is no market, but there is no market because there is no product. Even so,these new batteries are being put through their paces on a shoestring, for which we will someday be grateful, and from which, hopefully, some of the adventuresome small companies will get rich.

For reasons I cannot entirely grasp, Ford persists in developing its proprietary sodium-sulfur technology, even after having abandoned it in frustration twenty years ago, and Chrysler is betting on nickel-iron, a tree that Edison went around and around eighty years ago. Much publicity was created on October 25, 1991, by the announcement of a public-private merger of R&D efforts among GM, Ford, Chrysler, and the federal government. The total dollar volume committed to that new cooperative enterprise was $260 million, of which the Big Three were to contribute $100 million, over a period of five years. Unfortunately, the gesture is not as grand as it seems at first glance. Most manufacturing companies typically spend 3–4 percent of their total revenues on R&D. IBM spends 8 percent. GM's share of the $100 million, on an annual basis, represents a mere 0.015 percent of its sales volume, only about 4 percent of their R&D efforts.

Why hasn't our society put more of an effort into developing batteries? One persistent myth holds that all the really good patents were bought up by Standard Oil and buried forever. More probably, it's a simple matter of economics. If oil is cheap and plentiful, who will put up with a system that peters out, as some early ones did, after only thirty or forty miles, takes overnight to charge, and burns up its batteries after one year? This was the best the electric cars of the sixties and seventies could do, and it made an indelible impression on the few consumers courageous enough to try. Those misguided ventures did more to delay the proliferation of good batteries and electric vehicles (EVs) than any oil-cartel conspiracy.

A system of batteries running electric motors is the only technology available today that will meet the California and Massachusetts zero-emission criteria. To sell any cars in those states (and in others soon to follow) the automakers will have to play along, like it or not. If, by 1998, one automaker cannot meet the 2 percent standard zero-emission vehicle (ZEV) sales ratio, it may have to buy ZEV credits from the others, certainly an onerous and humiliating thing for any executive to contemplate.

Even boat manufacturers are dimly aware of the coming change, but they feel no pressure to conform. Their magic cloak of invisibility has shielded them from the basilisk gaze of public disapproval and regulatory government action.

An argument often raised against electric propulsion is that batteries still have to be charged by a power plant, thereby giving the lie to the term "zero emission," and accomplishing little but to shift the pollution problem elsewhere. While this is technically true, the argument ignores economies of scale: power plants, even including the coal-fired ones, are so much cleaner on average than internal combustion engines that, mile for mile, the average car today produces over 200 times more pollution than the electricity to power a ZEV, according to figures from the U.S. Department of Energy's Lawrence Livermore Laboratory.*

Ironically, electric vehicles are being fought bitterly—by environmentalists. Trying to counter the automotive lobby has proven to be a quixotic effort for concerned citizens. Not only must the battle be fought on a national scale at enormous expense, but it appears to threaten one of our most cherished American life-style perquisites: the personal automobile, and its unrestricted use.

Power-plant projects, on the other hand, can be successfully stopped by concerted efforts of grass-roots community and regional groups. With their seeming fondness for blighting the waterways to obtain limitless quantities of cooling water, their resistance to smoke scrubbing, and their unsightly monolithic architecture, power plants have become the *bête noire* of the environmental movement.

Because electric vehicles may create a demand for more power plants, they are seen as highly suspect. The utilities themselves, of course, like the idea. They see EVs as a means of creating demand for electricity during off-peak hours. Millions of batteries would be charging in the small hours of the night when power plants are normally idling wastefully.

Architecture notwithstanding, and the unfortunate history of heavy-handed power-plant proliferation, most utilities are now miles ahead of the rest of us, turning away from building more facilities and following the path of least resistance: conservation. One kilowatt-hour saved by a consumer's efficiency is one less kilowatt-hour of power plant that has to be built. And it costs a lot less.

I am partial to electricity as a marine fuel. I have experience with it, I understand its technologies, and I am confident that it can be effective, with all its limitations, today.

* Brooks, 1991.

But there is one overriding reason for liking electricity: universality of distribution.

No other energy source is as widespread or familiar as electricity. Therefore, when evaluating the likelihood of achieving global acceptance for clean power technologies, electricity is clearly the most practical energy source. An electric car or an electric boat can be "filled up" in Thailand, Egypt, Sweden, and Venezuela just as easily as it can be filled up in New York or San Francisco. It will be a long time, and a lot of scarce money, before the same can be said for ethanol, methanol, or natural gas.

Fuel Cells

Batteries, with all their limitations, are not the only source of propulsion electricity. Fuel cells actually produce energy on demand, on board. A fuel cell is "an electrochemical device that continuously converts the chemical energy of a fuel (and oxidant) to electrical energy."[*] Fuel cells generally come in modular "stacks" or "layers," composed of alternating sandwiches of coolant, fuel electrode, electrolyte matrix, air electrode, and separator.

Batteries are self-contained, and obtain their energy by receiving an electrical charge which "resets" the electrochemical balance within. In a fuel cell, however, an oxidant, usually air, and a reactant, or fuel, pass through the cell and are replenished from an outside source as they are consumed. Because they are not subject to limitations that characterize thermal machines, such as internal combustion engines or steam power plants, they offer the potential for extremely efficient conversion of energy.[†]

[*] Linden, 1984.
[†] Antonoff, 1991; IEEE, 1991a, b; Parish et al., 1989; Wills, 1991.

Happily, size is not a consideration; small cells operate nearly as efficiently as large ones. Fuel cells (FCs) have demonstrated conversion efficiencies (the ratio of input energy from one medium to energy available as output) as high as 70 percent, versus typical combustion engine efficiencies of less than 30 percent. The theoretical efficiency of FCs rises to 80 or 90 percent when process heat is recovered for use.*

Although the theory of FCs was in place 150 years ago, they did not become a reality until United Technologies engineer William Podolny, with the benefit of modern chemical and metals engineering, designed a model suitable for practical use. Workable units based on his design powered U.S. Gemini and Apollo space missions in the 1960s. Since then, Fuji, Westinghouse, United Technologies, Hitachi, and a number of equally high-powered European players have been in a headlong race to perfect FC technology for markets such as residential and industrial power generating as well as transportation and aerospace.

Utilities in Japan, Europe, and to a lesser degree in the United States are backing pilot projects. The implications are profound: with space at a premium in the inner cities, and with conventional power generators becoming increasingly difficult to build, a clean, silent, and doubly efficient on-site system, running on established natural gas infrastructures, a system that is flexible enough to power one single house or the World Trade Center, will be a sure bet to dominate power generation markets soon after achieving technical and economic viability. A small number of shops, hospitals, hotels, communications stations, and other commercial enterprises have already installed fuel cells as backup power instead of diesel generators.

Fuel cells are expected to make a strong debut in this decade. But it won't happen tomorrow, and the names of

* Romano and Price, 1990.

the FC technologies themselves express very eloquently the challenges faced in development: *phosphoric acid* fuel cells, *molten carbonate* fuel cells, *solid oxide* fuel cells, *proton exchange membrane* fuel cells—there isn't a friendly sounding name among them.

The electrolytes are one of the primary distinguishing characteristics: phosphoric acid, molten lithium, sodium and potassium carbonate, and solid zirconium oxide stabilized with yttrium oxide.* You won't find many starry-eyed kitchen chemists fooling around with these materials.

While fuel cells are widely considered to be very promising for transportation applications, few have found their way into terrestrial vehicles. One group of engineers from Georgetown University has conducted a thorough simulation of a phosphoric acid fuel cell in an urban transit bus, comparing performance projections from a number of different routes.†

They soon concluded that the bus would have to be outfitted with standard batteries for acceleration and hill climbing because thermal inertia (lag in time for the cell to convert fuel to electricity on demand) limits peak power ratings. They chose a methane-fueled 50-kilowatt phosphoric acid unit, roughly equivalent to 67 horsepower, for the small, twenty-three-passenger low-floor bus platform used in the simulation, augmented by another 50 kilowatts of available battery power. All indications were that such a bus would be completely satisfactory, and comparative emissions projections ranged from 1/250th of IC engine hydrocarbons to an infinitesimal 1/5,400th of IC engine NOx. A very impressive performance, even if only on paper.

We must wait to pass judgment on marine fuels until we understand the propulsion systems they will power. Armed

* Itoh, 1990.
† Romano and Price, 1990.

with a new body of knowledge about fuels, we can now consider the engines that will be consuming our fuels and moving our boats—always remembering, of course, the evaluation criteria we set forth. Primary among these criteria is low emissions, but practical real-time application and reasonable cost are also essential.

5

Clean Power

Wind

THE CLEANEST READILY ACCESSIBLE power is that of the wind. More than a million people go sailing every year. But the wind, after all, is fickle; sometimes here, sometimes gone, sometimes too soft, sometimes too hard, and always, it seems, coming toward you from the very direction you want to go. Long hours of numbing boredom are violently punctuated by moments of sheer terror. The eyes of your precious little family stare up at you through a companionway suddenly tilted over at 45 degrees. Squall howling overhead and sails flogging like a stampede of elephants, they are a family of little animals trapped in their burrow. "Dad! Is this all right?" Still, there are many people who thrive on those challenges, whose greatest pleasure in life is to harness the power of the wind.

I prefer to sail multihulls. There is no greater thrill than to harness the incredible power of a big catamaran in a strong breeze, to feel it accelerate like a sports car and fly across the water at 15, 20, 25 knots, and even more, with spray everywhere striking your body with the force of a fire hose. The miles spin out from under the lee transom, and the windward hull just kisses the tops of the waves, eerily smooth underfoot as the helmsman looks downwind at the chaos, noise, and weltering water around the leeward hull. It is the supreme sustained razor-edge mastery of ungovernable elements, all yielding the reward of speed, greater than any other sport that is readily accessible to the weekend warrior.

But relaxing it ain't. Nor is it practical—although it has its practical elements, as we will see in the next chapter on power multihulls.

In the 1970s, concurrent with the wooden boat revival, there was a strong surge of interest in the potential for practical commercial sailing craft. How splendid to sail, and have a rational excuse for doing it. "All this, and I get *paid*—?"

There is a great potential for sails and wind power to enhance the efficiency of powered pleasure boats. I once leaned spellbound against the rail of a big yacht I was cruising aboard, in port at Rockland, Maine, watching the maneuvers of an open boat with a single short mast amidships from which swung a three-bladed wind turbine. In a 10-knot breeze that was blowing away the fog that had imprisoned us at the dock, this amazing craft—did it sail, or did it power?—could go 4 or 5 knots directly into the eye of the wind.

I am sorely tempted to discuss here the many developments in sail-assisted power vessels, like the wind turbine, the Flettner rotor, and various computer-optimized automated sailing rigs that can greatly increase a powered vessel's efficiency,* but to do the subject justice would require a book all its own. So with apologies to those who would have liked to see it tackled here, I bend to the numbers: the weight of a million sailors is overwhelmed by the weight of 12 million powerboaters.

* Bergeson, 1981.

And their 12 million engines, after all, are the root of the pollution problem.

Invisible Refinements

Most of us know a few things about engines; we know about pistons and crankshafts, and anyone who has owned a car knows about spark plugs, coolant, alternators, and of course gasoline. The advent of the everyday automobile—2.1 of them in every driveway—has turned the complex science of internal combustion technology into pop-culture iconography. Advertising and pop media program us with the shiny curves of cars and perfect people driving, showing off, or making love in cars. Radio talk shows are dedicated to the art of automotive diagnosis, and hundreds of columnists and journalists across the country make a living satisfying the driving public's thirst for information. Words like "ignition," "exhaust," "intake," and "gasket" are almost universally familiar.

Not so familiar is a new generation of engine refinement technologies now entering the marketplace after years of development. The catalytic converter and electronic ignition are old friends, but others, such as the reverse-regeneration wall-flow honeycomb monolith particulate filter and the Nebula double-vortex swirl combustion chamber with plain-sided piston bowl, might need a little explanation.

Despite loud protests to the contrary,* most of the advances in internal combustion (IC) engine design over the last two decades have closely followed criteria and specification goals established by various governmental agencies in a process known as "technology-forcing." There is nothing new in this concept. The industrial revolution's early coal-burning technologies were sharply curtailed by governmental reac-

* GM, 1991a, b; NMMA, 1988–1991.

tions prompted by the public outcry after, among other things, the publication of Charles Dickens's *Hard Times* in the 1860s:

> Coketown lay shrouded in a haze of its own, which appeared impervious to the sun's rays. You only knew the town was there because there could be no such sulky blotch upon the prospect without a town. A blur of soot and smoke, now confusedly tending this way, now that way . . . a dense formless jumble, with sheets of cross light in it, that showed nothing but masses of darkness.

In fact, the first known "clean air act" may have been in 1306, when King Edward I of England banned the burning of "sea coles"—chunks of coal found, like driftwood, along the seashore.*

Engines—From Gunpowder to Gasoline

That smoky industrial revolution was the breeding ground of the internal combustion engine. It was not long before the steam engine was modified for a more direct transfer of energy by explosion inside the cylinders. Christiaan Huygens, whose contributions to science lay in the field of astronomy, built the first IC engine in 1680. It was fueled by exploding gunpowder. History tells us that it was used (with mixed success) in 1690 to pump water over a paddle wheel in a boat, thus dating the motorboat far earlier than the automobile.

One century later Robert Street, an Englishman, patented an engine that burned turpentine in its cylinders, again to pump water. Samuel Brown ran a coal-gas–fueled IC-powered 36-foot vessel on the Thames in 1832 for the Lords of the Admiralty. It seemed reliable, and paddled along at 7–8 knots decades before the first functioning car would see

* French, 1990.

the light of day. Predictably, the admiralty, while lauding the achievement, could think of no practical use for it.

In 1859, at the same time that Edward Drake was drilling his Pennsylvania well, Siegfried Marcus was at work in his German machine shop, building one of the seminal internal combustion engines. It had a single cylinder and ran for twenty minutes. After several years of tinkering, Marcus introduced the machine at the Vienna Exposition of 1875 by running it steadily for an unprecedented three hours.

Pierre Lenoir was also at work, in Paris, designing an engine that was practical. Built by Hippolyte Marinoni in 1860, it was essentially a steam engine with its power stroke propelled by an *in situ* explosion instead of pressurized steam, a blueprint that has been followed and elaborated on to this day. Lenoir's fuel was coal gas. Within five years 400 of his engines had been sold to drive stone cutters, polishers, printing presses, and lathes. His machine soon found its way into a boat that ran a regular route along the Seine River— the first practical motorboat.

Nikolaus Otto would borrow much of Lenoir's and Marcus's thinking to help develop his own four-cycle engines, leading to a patent in 1876, the first to become commercially successful.

By 1885, after an apprenticeship in the Deutz shops of Nikolaus Otto, Gottlieb Daimler was secretly testing his revolutionary 1.5-horsepower engine in a launch named the *Marie* on the Neckar River near Cannstatt, Germany.

Dugald Clerk developed two-cycle engines in England, and by 1881 he had developed a technique for pressurizing the fuel-air mix in one cylinder and transferring it to the main cylinder for ignition. For many years all two-stroke motors were referred to as "Clerk-cycle engines." Many found their way into boats.

Clerk's fuel-mix injection was forgotten until recently. That principle now goes by the high-tech name of EBDI (external breathing direct injection), and after 100 years of dirty two-cycle engines, it is the cornerstone of a new breed of cleaner two-strokes under development in Australia, the United States, and Japan.*

American Clark Sintz demonstrated an explosion-engine launch on the waters of a Michigan lake in 1885. His engine was unique because it featured, for the first time, a revolutionary apparatus that allowed a driver to adjust the exact moment of explosion inside to the cylinder to accommodate the different firing demands of cruising, accelerating, and cold-starting: ignition advance. In the same year, Karl Benz's prototype three-wheeled horseless carriage also featured electrical ignition (without advance), the first known carburetor, and recirculating water cooling.†

William Steinway's piano factory in New York was the unlikely site of further boat engine development. Steinway became enthralled with the ideas of Otto alumnus Wilhelm Maybach, who had come to America to visit his brother at the piano shops. By 1888 Steinway had negotiated exclusive American rights to an engine that was being built jointly by Maybach and Daimler. He could see the German engine's great potential, and decided to introduce it to the wealthy of America in pleasure boats.

His piano factory and craftsmen adapted easily to boatbuilding. Elegant Steinway launches up to 50 feet long, powered by twin Daimler 12-horsepower engines, cost as much as $7,000 in 1894. But, like many self-assured entrepreneurs to follow him, Steinway soon found that boatbuilding was not as easy as it had first seemed, and was causing him, despite assets of $20 million, "serious apprehensions as to monetary outlook." At his death in 1896, the courts declared Steinway's Daimler investment of $181,100 to be utterly worthless, and the piano factory terminated its boatbuilding efforts.‡ Today, of course, the Daimler-Benz

* Caprio, 1991.
† Clarke, 1984.
‡ Fostle, 1988.

Corporation is a multibillion-dollar business manufacturing Mercedes-Benz automobiles, trucks, and large marine diesels—but not boats. Steinway remains, wisely and profitably, in the piano business.

Turn-of-the-century steam engines could barely wring a single horsepower of work from hundreds of pounds of machinery, but the early IC engines were soon attaining power-to-weight ratios of 1 horsepower to a mere 35 pounds. Flouting the hundreds of patents that covered every aspect of IC engine development, small local builders from the most remote seacoast villages of Maine to the inland lakes country began to produce engines of their own.

A simple foundry and basic machine shop could build motors for sale to local boatmen at a cost of $100—a good part of a year's income, but an investment that so boosted productivity that most fishermen converted from sail or oar to power within a very few years. Before the "one-lunger" came along, a lobsterman could handle about twenty traps per day. Under power that number could triple, and give the fisherman's boat range to cover territory that had never been accessible before.*

Most of the one-lungers were two-cycle engines, with an explosion driving every stroke of the piston. These engines did not require valves, timing belts, and camshafts, so were much cheaper to build, simpler to maintain, and more reliable. The only moving parts in the powertrain were the piston, connecting rod, and crankshaft. They were massively built of cast iron, with poured lead bearings and easily fabricated parts.

Often known as "make-and-break" (after a system of internal cylinder-activated ignition contacts) and "hit-or-miss" (because of a fuel-conserving ignition governor that missed firing on alternate strokes when the engine was not under load), one-lungers survive today in prodigious quan-

---

* Seideman, 1992.

tities. Summertime county fairs all across America resound to the erratic staccato of these ancient engines.

As we all know, American engine and vehicle construction, once served by a profusion of competing builders, eventually shook down to four car companies; and now there are only three. When Henry Ford raised the ante for industrialized societies by paying his laborers the extravagant daily wage of $5, he not only paved the way for the emergence of a powerful working middle class but sounded the funeral dirge for a host of small mechanical fabricators. By the 1920s labor costs were too high for a small operation to compete with mass production. Markets glutted with overproduced commodities forced prices ever lower.* Modified versions of automotive engines became widely available, and dirt cheap.

By the early 1960s the internal combustion engine had attained the basic form we still see today. The V-8 had largely supplanted other formats, like the straight-12, straight-8, straight-6, straight-4, V-6, and V-12. Engine development tended to concentrate on power alone until the first federal Clean Air Act of 1963, although General Motors claims to have been interested in the environment since 1959.†

California laws established precedents for federal law then, and today they have done so again, three decades later. By demanding positive crankcase ventilation, then the source of 20 percent of automotive emissions, and the easiest source to quickly eliminate, in 1961 California set the standard that Washington would follow two years later.

Today the emissions-control issue is far more complex. Technology-forcing has caused a resurgence of smaller, high-efficiency engines in formats long deemed unacceptable for the American market: the V-6 and straight-4. Popular in Europe and Japan, where fuel has always been an expen-

* Hounshell, 1984.
† GM, 1991a.

sive, imported commodity, these newly sophisticated engines now power most cars on American streets. They incorporate features such as fuel injection, balance shafts, dual over-head camshafts pushing four valves per cylinder, combustion chamber vortices and swirl design, electronic engine management systems for precisely optimized timing and combustion, turbochargers, and catalytic emissions converters. Power-to-weight ratios of 1:2 (horsepower to pounds) are becoming common. Power output is rising, and so is unit fuel economy, as emissions are dwindling.

In cars. Not boats.

"It Can't Be Done" —Or Can It?

Efficiency of an engine is generally measured by evaluating five interrelated criteria: fuel consumption, power, weight, cost, and emissions. I would add a sixth: practicability. If a 500-horsepower engine that weighs 10 pounds, costs $200, uses teacups of fuel, and emits nothing won't work in a boat, or isn't available yet, then it cannot even be considered. Practicability has been one of the crutches the pleasure boat industry has leaned on while making its case against clean, efficient power. That, and the issue of cost.

"How," they ask, "can we possibly outfit our engines with catalytic converters when they all run wet exhaust"—exhaust cooled by the injection of engine-cooling "raw" water from outside the boat? "How can we use EMS [engine management system] and fuel injection when the cost increases will kill our competitive price edge?" "Our customers don't want that stuff—and they don't want to pay for it."

These are the same arguments that were used for decades by the automotive industry. The adoption of technology-forcing silenced (outwardly) the complaints, and allowed engineers to achieve the remarkable advances that have been seen in the last ten years, laying the groundwork for more remarkable changes to come.

How do powerboat propulsion systems measure up against the defining parameters of efficiency?

We have already looked at pleasure boating's voracious lust for fuel. Abysmal fuel mileage is caused by three factors: operator habits, the high torque requirements of most present-day powerboats, and the atavistic character of pleasure boat engines. A family automobile may well travel 25 miles on the energy contained in a gallon of gasoline, but the same family's boat will travel only 2 miles. Boaters, we have seen, have been trained by the industry to "need" high speeds and lots of unused horsepower.

And it is true that the boats designed for these boaters do need unbelievable amounts of power to push them along.

Today's family automobile, once on the highway and cruising, might need only 30 horsepower to maintain 60 miles per hour. The family boat, on the other hand, does not enjoy the benefits of a gearbox that allows the engine to loaf along while the car cruises. The boat's engine moves the boat as a linear function of its rpm's. If the propeller math says the prop must be rotating 3,500 times per minute to move the boat 35 miles per hour, then the engine, in most cases, must also be revolving at a rate of 3,500 times per minute. If that engine redlines at, say, 4,000 or 4,200 rpm's, then the motor is developing most of its available horsepower all the time.

One of the most obvious ways to improve boat fuel economy is, therefore, to improve the efficiency of the energy transfer from engine to water. The motor must rotate slower, the propeller must be more effective, the boat must have less friction with the water and air it is moving through.

Boat engines already develop plenty of power; they are known for it. After Detroit's much-publicized (and largely fictional) discontinuance of the V-8 engine, thousands of disappointed hot rodders across the nation had nowhere to turn for performance engines. Nowhere, that is, except to the unregulated boat industry. Many a drag racer is still nursing along an engine bought from Mercruiser or Crusader in the late 1970s and early 1980s. Today that handoff is going the other direction, as uninterested boat engine builders work with whatever engines Detroit sends them, primitive or advanced.

Outboard motors, as the exclusive province of the pleasure boating industry, are an exception. Despite the opprobrium being heaped upon them in these pages, outboards are beautifully compact wonders of concentrated power in astonishingly lightweight packages. A typical top-of-the-line 200-horsepower V-6 or V-8 outboard motor operates at a power-to-weight ratio that approaches 1:1, lower unit, shafting, and propeller included. Two-stroke racing motorcycle engines of 500-cubic-centimeter displacement (equivalent to 30 cubic inches, or 0.5 liter) are now producing 130 horsepower, and if efficiency were measured by power-to-weight or power-to-displacement ratios alone, two-strokes would be the clear winners. They can be beautifully engineered for compactness, simplicity, profound power output,and reliability.*

Unfortunately, despite advances in oil injection and crankcase fuel scavenging (internal recirculating), they still burn more fuel than an equivalent big-block V-8, and they still pollute 140 times worse than a car, and every year pump the lion's share of 400,000,000 gallons of oil and toxic hydrocarbons into the air and water we all depend on for life.

New technology being developed jointly by Mercury and Chrysler, and by Ford, GM, and OMC, however, holds great promise for housebreaking the incontinent two-cycle engine, although marketable products are still many years away. Because the two-stroke has such tremendous power den-

* Brown, personal communication, 1990.

sity, it has the potential to dominate future transportation if—and it's a very big "if"—fuel consumption and emissions can be brought into line.

External breathing direct injection (EBDI), Chrysler's two-stroke project, has the potential to achieve these goals. With only 15 moving parts (versus 200 for a comparable four-stroke), prototype EBDIs point the way toward smaller, cheaper engines doing more work, thus consuming less fuel, and producing fewer emissions. An appealing prospect.

Proponents of the Orbital two-stroke engine, currently in the prototype stage at Ford, say that hydrocarbon emissions can be reduced by as much as 90 percent—comparable to an unregulated four-stroke engine—and cite very low NOx emissions. They also claim comparable fuel mileage from a power package that will eventually be simpler, lighter, and cheaper. Orbital engines still, however, lubricate on the "total-loss" principle of their dirtier predecessors, unlike Chrysler's EBDI engine.

John German* at EPA in Ann Arbor says that the Orbital engine is not yet working as a mass-producible entity. So many things have to happen inside the cylinder in the minuscule amount of time provided by one single stroke that the engine's potential has yet to be realized.

Best estimates are that the first engines will be entering the general market in five or more years, although a natural conversion of the outboard motor market may take another decade. A discouraging indication of the industry's attitude toward the Orbital and EBDI technology was the two-stroke engine's complete absence from the 1992 auto shows, where anything even remotely feasible is mocked up and displayed. There were sodium-sulfur batteries and hydrogen fuel tanks—but no two-strokes.

A big-block (7-liter) engine, complete with gear (transmission) or sterndrive, weighs about 1,200 pounds, and

---

* German, personal communication, 1992.

produces an average 300 horsepower at the propeller. Its power-to-weight ratio is therefore 1:4. A small-block V-8 (5.7-liter) generally puts about 230 horsepower into the water, and weighs 900 pounds, and the power-to-weight ratio is comparable. A marinized Mazda rotary engine, on the other hand, is rated at 175 horsepower and weighs only 350 pounds, for a ratio of 1:2. By the measure of power-to-weight, it is therefore twice as power efficient as a conventional V-8 or V-6.

The Mazda engine will burn 7 gallons per hour when cruising. If a twin-rotary setup were compared with a single V-8 of comparable power, the rotaries would use about 14 gallons per hour and the V-8 would use 20. Therefore, the rotary Wankel configuration is more fuel efficient. (There are some questions about the Mazda's practicability, it should be noted. While no one is actually saying as much, widespread distribution of the rotary for pleasure boat use is being delayed because of concerns over the engine's ability to withstand long-term high torque loadings.)

A big question in my mind is this: Why haven't we seen any of the new high-output fours and sixes, which are running so successfully in nine out of ten automobiles we buy today, outfitted for marine use?

A fuel-injected turbocharged four-cylinder engine with high compression and dual-cam 16-valve heads will develop over 200 horsepower and weigh only 200 pounds, 250 with gear—close to the power efficiencies of outboard motors. Even when subjected to high torque loadings, such an engine will consume less than one gallon of gasoline for every 20 miles driven hard on a dynamometer—3 gallons per hour. In a boat outfitted with two such engines, easy cruising speeds of 25 mph could be achieved for a total fuel consumption rate of 4.5 gallons per hour—more than twice as fuel efficient as a conventional V-8, all other conditions being the same.

If a four-cylinder engine isn't tough enough (though all

indications are to the contrary), what about motors such as the GM 4.3-liter V-6, which powers cars, light trucks, and even heavy delivery vans? That engine, currently undergoing natural gas operation testing in a California UPS fleet, can be turbocharged and high-outputted to more than compete with any V-8 in power, and go a lot farther on the same gallon of fuel.

It is clear that significant improvements in efficiency are available to anyone interested in applying them to pleasure boats. Still, no builders are interested because they think they can't afford to take the risks, and the industry is convinced that its customers don't care. But has it asked them? I have my doubts.

Taming Exhaust Emissions

Exhaust emissions control is the area where the most quantitative progress has been made toward propulsive efficiency—in cars. Not boats. The fuel mileage of an average family car has gone from 14 to 20 miles per gallon over the last two decades, a healthy 43 percent improvement, and emissions have declined to 4 percent of 1970 levels, a 25-fold improvement, and they are slated to decline even farther. A remarkable achievement.

The average car in 1967 was "uncontrolled," and had emission levels of 15–17 grams of hydrocarbons per mile. This is the epoch that pleasure boat engines are, for the most part, stuck in. Today the standard for cars is 0.25 gram per mile, moving toward 0.075 gram per mile. How has this miracle been achieved? And why has it not been mirrored by equivalent progress in the marine industry?

A combination of parallel efforts has resulted in tremendous emission reductions from internal combustion engines. Fuel injection has proven to be a finely controllable medium, allowing engineers to manage precise control of fuel flows under the dauntingly diverse array of conditions engines typically operate under, thus eliminating fuel waste and helping optimize combustion.* Turbochargers and exhaust gas recirculation boost power output by approximately 25 percent, and recycle about 10 percent of the exhaust gases back into the combustion chambers under pressure, where improved flame propagation improves combustion and some of the unburned hydrocarbons are consumed.

Sophisticated combustion chamber geometry helps to ensure that the entire charge of fuel and air is consumed during the burn cycle. (The Nebula system mentioned earlier, by the way, is a unique multiple vortex combustion swirl configuration developed by Ricardo Consulting Engineers, Ltd. Unburned charge from crevices in the combustion chamber, such as piston ring and gasket crevices, produces 25–50 percent of all hydrocarbon emissions. Flame-quenching, a condition of poor burning at the far edges of the combustion chamber, contributes 8–10 percent of total hydrocarbon emissions. Nebula, and many other designs, combat these conditions.†)

Spark-plug location, multiple spark plugs, swirl and vortex configurations, shape of cylinder top, intake and exhaust efficiency, which is usually enhanced by multiple-valving and computer-modeled gas routing, and manipulation of the rich / lean (equivalence) ratio all help to make the IC explosion as mighty and complete as possible. These processes are controlled by electronics in a "black box" called an engine management system (EMS).‡

The EMS continuously reads data being fed to it from the fuel system, the exhaust system, the engine, the ignition system, the coolant, the valve train, and from the operator's input. It understands timing, temperature, flow, speed, and

* Niesen, personal communication, 1992.

† Dempster and Shore, 1990.

‡ Downham, personal communication, 1991; Schmidt, personal communication, 1992.

status, and is programmed to make its decisions based upon the input to vary timing, fuel flow, exhaust flow, burn rate, and other elements that contribute to the desired result: optimum clean combustion.

Even motor oil must be selected with caution. Multi-viscosity oils commonly contain styrene-butadiene viscosity index improvers, which find their way into the exhaust.*

Many engineers just congenitally hate exhaust gas aftertreatment. They cite catalyst-generated rhodium and platinum components in exhaust gas analyses, and say that given enough time they will be able to meet federal emission standards without it. Still, the catalytic converter remains, from my point of view, the chief miracle of them all.

A catalyst, in the field of chemistry, is a chemical compound that accelerates the rate of a chemical reaction without being consumed itself.† In catalytic converters metals coated with reactant compounds work by absorbing the flowing gases into their surface, forming intermediate compounds that readily react to form the desired product, and then forming that product while regenerating the original surface of the catalyst.

An exhaust catalyst is typically a densely packed honeycomb of thin precious metal leaves (platinum, silver, palladium, or rhodium) through which exhaust gas flows on its way to the tail pipe. When cold, it is inert. But when light-off temperature (approximately 600°F) has been reached after a few minutes of driving, the reactant coating on the metal surfaces causes elements of the exhaust to change character. As the gases move past the surfaces of the catalyst they are chemically altered by the reactant and the heat into other compounds. Carbon monoxide, for instance, is altered to

* Pelz et al., 1990.
† Clarke, 1984.

form carbon dioxide and water vapor. The reactant coating is tailored by the manufacturer to convert as many of the target compounds as possible into benign molecules.

The most difficult challenge for catalyst development seems to be the mutually exclusive catalyzation characteristics of hydrocarbons and oxides of nitrogen. NOx is a potent greenhouse gas (and a big contributor to acid rain), hydrocarbons are carcinogenic, and together they form the air toxins known as smog. Catalyst "tuning" to eliminate one encourages an increase in the other. Most hydrocarbons are virtually eliminated by a three-way catalytic converter, although methane, one of the simplest, is particularly stubborn.

Catalysts also vary their behavior in different operating conditions—generally poorest at idle, when gases are coolest, and at full throttle or heavy torque loadings, and best at medium throttle settings or light load conditions—but in any case they provide diminished levels of harmful emissions, and on average account for two-thirds of the overall improvement in land vehicle emissions control.

So why aren't catalytic converters in boats? One reason is the cowboy factor: conservative boatbuilders and hopped-up boat buyers concerned with virility and machismo don't want 'em. Period. Another reason is the it-just-can't-be-done syndrome, the pathetic wail of impossibility that is raised whenever the subject comes up in boating industry circles. Most boat exhausts are "wet," the pundits protest, and catalysts need to be hot and dry. Another objection is cost. Converters cost the average car owner about $150, and marine installations might cost several times that amount.

Aside from cost (which is an issue in itself—should we be subsidizing low-cost dirty boat engines with the money we pay into the "social costs fund"?), the mechanical problems are straightforward enough to be solved easily. Engine exhaust would have to be routed upwards first, through a dry loop to the catalyst, and then back down to a water-injection point. To keep the catalyst chamber hot without endangering the boat or its occupants, the catalyst and the dry loop would have to be wrapped with insulation and kept isolated from sensitive systems or hull parts. EMS would take care of maintaining catalyst temperature through exhaust throttling, controlled catalyst ventilation, or gas dilution. Elevated backpressure caused by the gases having to get through a catalyst will rob only a small amount of power from the engine, and in a fully engineered clean-power propulsion system, which is likely to run stronger than a conventional one, the loss will not be noticed. Dry exhaust is another possibility, one which is in operation on thousands of workboats around the world.

Alternative fuels adapt well to IC applications, and their already cleaner "engine-out" emissions (directly from the engine, uncatalyzed) can be significantly reduced through the application of exhaust catalysts. The test of practicability will determine alternate fuel usage more than anything else. Methanol, ethanol, natural gas, and liquid petroleum gas are just not widely available yet. Technology-forcing is slowly changing the availability picture for land vehicles, however, and there is no reason to suppose the same thing can't happen for marine vehicles as well.

A typical family car is in operation approximately 500 hours per year (15,000 miles at an average speed of 30 mph). Most pleasure boats don't see that kind of use in three years. Therefore, catalysts can be expected to last 10–15 years, or more, in marine applications, which helps ease the pain of their cost.

Diesel—The Dark Horse

What of the diesel (compression-ignition) engine? Every year some 8,000–10,000 new diesel engines are sold for pleasure boat installations, closely reflecting sales at the upper end of that market. Anyone who has been stuck in traffic behind a smoking bus has ample reason to suspect that diesel emissions are going to be very difficult to control, but such is not necessarily the case.

Fuel and internal refinements similar to those I have described for spark-ignition engines are already being applied to the diesel, including the advent of engine management systems, with the result that particulates have been drastically reduced and crankcase hydrocarbon venting is now being captured in most cases. Problems that remain to be overcome are the emission of sulfates originating from the high sulfur content of diesel fuel, the emission of particulates, which despite improvements are still a major problem, unburned hydrocarbons, polycyclic aromatics, aldehydes—and a lot of NOx.

On the good side, diesels operate with an oxygen surplus ("a lean exhaust condition"). Therefore, catalyst light-off comes readily, and because specific fuel consumption is lower than that of spark-ignition engines (0.38 pound per horsepower-hour for a Cummins diesel versus 0.55 pound per horsepower-hour for a Crusader 454 gasoline engine), carbon dioxide emissions are much lower as well. Diesel engines are the propulsion of choice for high-torque applications in industry and transportation. Their acceptance came relatively easily.

Rudolf Diesel, inventor of the compression-ignition engine that bears his name, was born into extreme poverty in 1858. He was a withdrawn, taciturn youth, but showed an aptitude for mechanical things. At school in France he became a specialist in refrigeration, and published his first paper on the internal combustion engine when he was twenty years old. His first efforts, into which he poured time and money, were directed toward an ammonia-gas—fueled engine. That work went unrewarded.

Eventually, however, he hit upon the idea of an engine fired by the extreme heat generated during compression of a gas, and in 1892 Diesel had patented an engine that used coal dust blown under pressure into the combustion chamber. The motor was cranky and unreliable, so his detractors duly claimed that compression-ignition was impossible despite, as is usual with detractors, the evidence before their very eyes.

Experiments with more versatile hydrocarbons, such as gasoline and what is now known as diesel fuel, were very promising, and by 1893 Diesel had the high-powered backing of Krupps-Essen and the MAN group. Fuel consumption proved to be about half that of the concurrent crop of spark engines, and this encouraged Diesel's backers to remain faithful despite years of battle with material and technical problems. By the turn of the century Diesel was becoming a wealthy man as his engines found more and more use in heavy industrial applications worldwide.

He came to the United States to market his invention and was successful here, but soon thereafter began to exhibit grandiose notions and embarrassing delusions. He set himself up as an oil speculator, in direct competition with Rockefeller, but his mental health deteriorated so severely that he had to be hospitalized. His business affairs disintegrated. When he disappeared from the channel steamer *Dresden* on the night of September 29, 1913, few people doubted that he had taken his own life in despair (although there were rumors of international intrigue and murder).*

Diesel's unfortunate ending notwithstanding, the engine he created has proved durable, and ubiquitous, I am sure, beyond his wildest dreams. It is found in locomotives, factories, heavy trucks, and buses, and for the same reasons in ships, tugboats, and larger pleasure boats. The compression-ignition engine has proven to be adaptable for really

* Mateucci, 1970.

enormous power requirements—such as those of million-barrel oceangoing supertankers. Big diesel engines are so huge they have to be assembled inside the very boat they will power. Several men can stand on top of one piston.

Diesel engines have proven to be very popular performers in pleasure boats. They provide strong, reliable, and safe power in sizes from 9–100 horsepower for sailing yachts to 100–2,000 horsepower for motor yachts of varying sizes and types. Despite a much higher initial cost, diesel power is often chosen over gasoline power because of safety—diesel fuel is not readily explosive or flammable—and economy of operation. The reason I hear most often is that gas engines of equivalent horsepower can't run at a fast cruise without opening up their four-barrel carburetors and inhaling 20, 25, or more gallons per hour, per engine, costing a great deal of money and greatly limiting the vessel's operating range. Diesels, being thrifty and fuel injected, have no such problem, cruising at 12–16 gallons per hour, per engine, *ceteris paribus.*

Almost all diesel engines for road transportation and recreational boating are now being equipped with turbochargers and aftercoolers, which boost power outputs into ranges comparable with conventional gasoline engines. Unit costs are daunting, however, often reaching three times the cost of a comparable gas-powered engine due to massive construction and extremely close tolerances. Despite their rugged and unassuming exteriors, most diesels are built like a Swiss watch on the inside. Still, many boat buyers are willing to pay two or three times the cost of a gasoline engine for the benefits of a diesel, giving the lie to industry pundits whining about the prohibitive costs of relatively minor improvements to spark-ignition engines.

Diesels come in two- and four-cycle configurations, each of which convey many of the same advantages and disadvantages as they do in a spark-ignition format. The two-stroke diesel, represented in this country most typically by the Detroit Diesel Company (DDC) 6V-71 and 6V-92 engines, fires on every piston stroke and has half the number of valves and tophamper as a four-cycle diesel. It produces a few more horsepower out of a given weight, which is an advantage,* but emits more pollution, which is a disadvantage. Cummins and Caterpillar engines are the dominant American four-cycle marine diesels, in head-to-head competition with Swedish Volvos and Japanese Yanmars. Mercruiser and OMC have both entered the diesel field with smaller engines for runabout or smaller cruiser applications, the same market that Volvo and Yanmar have had to themselves for a number of years. Perversely, every one of these diesel manufacturers is claiming to be *the* environmental engine—unlike gasoline engine manufacturers, who make an inherently cleaner product (so far) but are too unconcerned to promote it as such. Why?

Because all the marine diesels are modified truck engines, subject to a new, very stringent set of technology-forcing regulations. Unlike companies such as Mercruiser, Crusader, Volvo Penta, Yamaha, and OMC, who do not sell products for land vehicle application and couldn't care less about environmental regulations (with a few exceptions), the diesel builders are all direct suppliers of truck and bus engines. They are heavily invested in the day-to-day fight to meet a very stringent set of standards for 1994, and indeed to catch up on some 1991 inner-city standards that couldn't be met on time. They are fully involved in clean power and it's costing them a lot of money, so why shouldn't they spread out their development costs over more markets, like the boating industry? They are indeed trying.

Diesel engines will run on methanol, and there are hundreds of prototype methanol-fueled compression-ignition heavy utility vehicles in service around the country today. The first was a DDC-powered bus in Marin County, Cali-

* Tindall, personal communication, 1992.

fornia, which has been in operation since early 1984. Methanol diesels exhibit some good characteristics and some not so good. They emit lower levels of carbon monoxide, and much lower levels of NOx. Particulate levels are a mere 15 percent of those from a conventional-fuel diesel. Fuel economy, on a carbon-equivalency basis, is almost identical, although more gallons of methanol are required to do the job. The bad news is that formaldehyde emissions are much higher, as are total exhaust hydrocarbons (methane being a big component).* There are, however, catalysts that will reduce formaldehyde emissions to less than 3 percent of uncatalyzed levels.† That leaves methane emissions to be overcome by more sophisticated high-temperature catalyst technologies.

Diesel engines modified to ignite by spark are able to run effectively on natural gas, and although compressed natural gas emits plenty of methane too, the net quantity is significantly lower than that from methanol combustion. Coupled with exhaust aftertreatment, alternate-fueled diesels have the demonstrated ability to meet federal and California guidelines with existing technology. They must compete for cost effectiveness, however, with conventional diesels running on reformulated diesel fuel and outfitted with particulate traps or flow-through oxidation catalysts. High initial conversion costs to modify nondedicated alternate fuel engines will have to be weighed against the high anticipated costs of reformulated diesel fuel.

Standard diesel engines are achieving major emissions reductions through the use of a wide variety of catalysts, traps, and filters. The catalysts aim at an array of pollutants, and we have already discussed their basic operations and configurations, so there is little need to reiterate them here. Traps and filters, however, address the large quantities of

* Eberhard et al., 1990.
† Santoro et al., 1990.

carbon particulates that are the unique by-product of diesel engines burning diesel fuel. Because soot from diesel-powered trucks and buses is the single most visible source of urban air pollution, countries all around the world are conducting experiments with low-particulate aftertreatment systems.

In Athens, Greece, there is a fleet of 120 buses equipped with trap oxidizers. As described by Pattas and his colleagues,* engine exhaust passes through these traps and particulate matter is deposited on porous ceramic monoliths as it passes through the walls of the ceramic. As one can easily imagine, the filter element soon becomes clogged and creates excessive backpressure, which can destroy the efficiency and power of the motor. The system must therefore possess the capacity to "regenerate" itself—to burn off the carbon particles and start again. How often this happens depends on fuel quality, motor type and condition, vehicle duty cycle, and the trap's construction.

The Athenian design utilizes an electronic control unit, similar to an engine EMS, that monitors temperature, flow, and backpressure. When backpressure reaches a predetermined level the black box concludes that it is time for a regeneration. The flow of exhaust gas to the filters is reduced by throttling valves, causing temperatures inside the four trap elements to rise to ignition temperatures. By measuring pressure differentials between exhaust entry and exit points, the black box knows when regeneration is complete and restores normal exhaust flows. If temperatures inside the traps rise above a predetermined level at any time, the controller automatically diverts all the exhaust gases to a bypass loop, allowing the elements to cool off. The filter elements are made by NGK of Japan and by Corning in the United States.

---

* Pattas et al., 1990.

To ensure a complete burnoff the Athenians add cerium naphthenate to their fuel in concentrations ranging from 25 ppm to 150 ppm by weight. This organometallic compound is made in France, and has been selected because of its extremely low toxicity. Almost 100 percent of the cerium additive is retained in the filters as an ash after regeneration.

Filter elements had to be removed from the buses after about 30,000 kilometers of operation, but after air blasting and water washing they were returned to the buses and continued to function at better than 90 percent of their original capacity. After 45,000 kilometers they were replaced. Throttling (regeneration) operation occurred over less than 0.5 percent of total running time, and bypass occurred through only 1 percent of the total time. The city is so pleased with the results that they are outfitting an additional 150 buses with the system.

I have described the Greek design in some detail because it seems to be the most complete, effective, and thoroughly tested of all the systems currently in use, with a cumulative 2 million kilometers of service mileage. A Japanese paper* describes a typical team wrangling with problems such as filter thermal failure, which the Greeks have overcome with their bypass system.

The Japanese and many other researchers are attempting to optimize regeneration by initiating a burn with electric heating elements, a promising technique that has yet to reach its full potential. A group of Canadians is doing laboratory experiments with microwave irradiation as a means of better distributing the regeneration burn throughout a filter element.† An American group is experimenting with electrostatic agglomerators to remove soot, with an 80 percent

* Shinozaki et al., 1990.
† Walton et al., 1990.

capture rate. Their design will feature a centrifugal clean-ing device to spin out soot accumulations, and will obviate high-temperature regeneration.*

The combined effects of internal advances in engine and combustion efficiency with the successes of particulate traps lead one to conclude that very clean diesel installations in pleasure boats are both feasible and desirable. Particulate control has been a feature of the massive seagoing diesels in freighters and tankers for years.

Zero Emissions Means *Electricity*

By 1998 there *must* be ZEVs (zero-emission vehicles) and ULEVs (ultra-low emission vehicles) for sale and on the road in California and Massachusetts, and at the time of this writing twelve additional states have similar laws in the leg-islative pipeline. There is no internal combustion engine that has the capacity to meet ZEV standards, and only very sophisticated small alternate-fueled spark-ignition engines can meet TLEV (transitional low-emission vehicle) guide-lines, let alone ULEV. This seems to point toward a com-pelling need for electric and hybrid propulsion systems. What will these ZEV and ULEV systems look like? Will they work in pleasure boats?

Today it seems as if ZEVs—zero-emission vehicles—will be propelled by rechargeable battery-powered electric sys-tems, and ULEVs by hybrid systems, which use a small steady-state (constant-speed) IC engine-driven generator to supplement the energy available from the batteries. While the hardware for electric propulsion—motors, control cir-cuits, and drives—is all ready to go, and has been since Jen-atzy's time, the stumbling block remains energy storage.

Gasoline is 50 times more energy-dense than lead-acid

* Thimsen et al., 1990.

battery power, by weight. Cost per mile is about the same, which gives some idea of the potential for electric propulsion, but customary operating ranges have been difficult to achieve because of excess weight and poor energy density. Despite battery problems, it is worth taking a look at the workings of electric propulsion to see the great potential for clean power applications—many of which are feasible today.

Electric propulsion comes in two basic formats: AC and DC. DC is the simplest to develop, but ultimately falls below AC in overall efficiency. The components involved in a typical electric propulsion system are:

- The energy source (batteries, fuel cell, generator).
- Power electronics (the "fuel system").
- Control electronics (speed and direction control).
- Diagnostic electronics (gauges and senders).
- Charging system (manages battery charging).
- Bells and whistles (nonstandard features).
- The motor.
- The infrastructure (wire harnesses, fuses, and connectors).

Joe Fleming, president of the Elco boatbuilding company and former president of Ramsey Controls, a pioneer in AC motor controls, is fond of saying, "the three-phase AC induction motor is the simplest prime-mover mankind has ever developed." It has just one moving part, yet is capable of truly unlimited applications, and will operate at up to 97 percent efficiency. This means that for every 100 units of energy that get fed in, only 3 get lost to heat, and the rest come back out in the form of work. Compare this to the 20–30 percent efficiency of a normal internal combustion engine.

DC motors work very well in cars and boats. Elco, for instance, has used DC for all of its classic electric launches, and Duffield, in Newport Beach, California, also uses DC in its harbor cocktail launches. The control electronics are simpler, and thus easier to develop. Safe low-voltage applications, like boat systems, are much more feasible in DC, because off-the-shelf low-voltage DC components are readily available, although not cheap. AC components are much more prevalent in industry, however, and the big production runs typical of industrial electronics can dramatically lower component costs.

AC voltage ratings generally begin at 110 V, however, and that is a level many people consider potentially unsafe. For short-term development or low-volume production, DC is probably the best bet. For long-term thinking, where high production numbers are involved, AC is the favorite choice of power engineers.

A third, much-publicized type of electric propulsion is called "brushless DC." Batteries provide direct-current power, and the power electronics give it three-phase characteristics which allow the use of AC-type motors. These systems are to be found in most of the solar racecars. GM's Impact, which specifies AC induction motors, batteries, and dual MOSFET inverters, is a brushless DC system, even though they don't bill it as such.

What is probably the most advanced electric motor available today has been created by Unique Mobility, Inc., of Denver, Colorado. Their brushless DC technology features an inner magnet ring and an outer magnet ring which encircle the fixed stator windings, and when used in conjunction with rare-earth magnets and polyphase stator windings the result is a high-density flux that produces 67 horsepower from a 42-pound motor.* It is not difficult to see, given specifications like these, why most developmental electric vehicle systems are using such equipment.

The best of motors and batteries, however, cannot run without switching and power-controlling devices to efficiently deliver variable speeds and reversing. The most

* Nelson, 1990.

sophisticated electric motor control electronics are called pulse-width-modulation systems. The electronics chop up the incoming power—digitize it—and feed it to the motor in gaps and pulses of millisecond durations. Speed is changed by shortening or stretching the length of the pulse, which remains at a constant current. Seen on an oscilloscope, a slow speed looks like a line of tiny dots, a medium speed looks like a row of dashes, and as speed is increased the dashes get longer and longer until they are a straight line at maximum power.*

Old electric propulsion systems regulated speed by picking up varying degrees of current from segmented battery banks, often with varying voltage, or even by cutting current with line resistance, all of which wasted power. These systems were used from the advent of electrical technology—people were still shooting buffalo from trains and occasionally fighting Native Americans in the Wild West when electricity was being showcased as the modern miracle at the Columbian Exposition of 1893—and even as recently as 1990 by an electric boat builder on the West Coast. Most cheap fishing trolling motors also use stone-age power controls. Coupled with the limitations of lead-acid batteries, outmoded power controls give electric propulsion a mixed reputation. These limitations need no longer apply to well-designed electric drive systems. Moreover, development of high-energy batteries is no longer a matter of "if," but a matter of "when," so it is important to consider that any electric boat with state-of-the-art electronics will be retro-fittable as new batteries come onto the market, increasing the boat's speed and range. We can expect fast, long-ranged electric boats within the next ten years, and sooner if the technology is forced by legislation.

Hybrid propulsion is even more feasible in the short term. In hybrid propulsion designs for cars, trucks, and buses, a

* Fleming, personal communication, 1988.

small IC generator powers the vehicle at cruising speeds, where energy demands are relatively low, and the batteries provide power surges for hill climbing or acceleration. The generator also keeps the batteries charged when descending or at rest, and regenerative braking provides an additional underway charging source.

The virtue of using a generator versus a variable-speed motor is this: when an engine runs at a constant speed it emits 30 percent fewer pollutants. It can also be mounted in isolation from the vehicle structure for very effective sound and vibration suppression.

Boats, of course, have unique requirements. The torque curve remains high at cruising speeds because of largely inescapable hydrodynamic resistances (which we will whittle away somewhat in the next chapter), and in all likelihood a marine hybrid system will be linked to a system-wide EMS-type control module. Depending on boat type, wind and sea conditions, and operator-variable factors, the EMS might pull 100 percent of available power from both sources, or it might need only 20 percent from the battery bank for propulsion and devote the generator to charging. Remember, only a small percentage of a pleasure boat's time at sea is spent at high speeds. Where the statistical power curve flattens out or dips, as it does, for example, in the duty cycle of a car or bus, it will also dip for boat operations because of long times at idle or subplaning speeds. In either case, the benefits are similar.

A hybrid system greatly enhances the overall energy density of electric propulsion. It will give much greater range or much greater speeds, or moderate amounts of both. It will offer an operator tremendous flexibility as well, giving him the ability to cruise slowly and silently, or more rapidly with the gentle hum of the generator below decks. In the not-too-distant future, fuel cells will replace generators as the fueled element of a hybrid system, cutting noise and emissions still further.

Electric propulsion may seem to be a poor choice for a watery environment, and poorly designed systems have indeed failed due to corrosion and moisture. Anybody who has owned an older boat must really question the sanity of a person extolling the virtues of electricity afloat. Today, however, we have many engineering advantages that were not available as recently as ten years ago. There are sealed gel-cell batteries, new sealants, corrosion-proof coatings, insulation materials, terminals, desiccants, and watertight enclosures and modules which simply did not exist before. With the advent of fiberglass, the interior of an average boat is much dryer than it was in the fifties and sixties.

And, curiously, electronic components are not damaged by total immersion in water. An AC motor, in fact, will run underwater. If an electronic motor or power control is flooded, it needs only to be flushed with fresh water to remove any dirt, grit, and salt, and then dried before it can be returned to service as good as new.* Atmospheric conditions don't affect operations at all, and I have driven electric boats through blinding downpours with no effects whatsoever on the strength or character of the power.

But then, at long last, the energy we have spent so much time fussing over and fine-tuning reaches the propeller—where it promptly loses 30, 40, 50, 60, even 70 percent to propeller inefficiency.

Rethinking the Propeller

These losses are not a big secret. Every propeller calculation table shows horrendous loss numbers in the normal range of propeller efficiencies. And worse still, those efficiencies are indicated for an optimum target speed range. At higher or lower speeds efficiencies are much lower.

* Fleming, personal communication, 1990.

Primitive propeller design and drive-train consideration are therefore one of the principal reasons why pleasure boats have to use such astronomical amounts of fuel (and produce the resultant emissions) to accomplish so little. Even leaving other things exactly as they are, I maintain that it is possible to cut overall pleasure boat emissions at least 30 percent just by redesigning and rethinking the propeller.

Whatever form of power is being employed, it must be delivered to the supporting medium with the lowest possible losses. If the vehicle is a car, losses (noticeable to the untrained eye as heat) will occur in the transaxle, universal joints, wheel bearings, and tires. On a boat, the losses will occur, similarly, in the marine gear (transmission), the stuffing box (a bearing where the propeller shaft exits the hull that allows the shaft to rotate without letting water in), shaft bearings, and propeller.

Killingly high overall losses of efficiency can easily creep into the system through these sources, destroying the value of much thoughtful work that may have gone into the rest of the drive train.

Motor manufacturers are now required to list their products' power ratings at the propeller instead of at the crankshaft. Transmissions eat up the lion's share of a typical 10 percent system-wide loss. Sterndrives make the axis of rotation take two 90-degree turns before delivering it to the propeller, outboards only one. Many inboard installations, particularly those in smaller, faster boats, use the Borg-Warner 71 and 72 series hydraulic transmissions, which rob 8–10 percent of an engine's power. The newer BW 5000-series gear has reduced energy losses to levels between 2 and 4 percent, comparable to mechanical gear transmissions. (It should be remembered that a marine transmission does not have several different available gear ratios the way an automotive transmission does. It provides a single ratio in forward, and a single ratio in reverse. The designer must choose the ratio that best suits a single "optimum" aspect of his boat's operating requirements. Outside of that narrow target range, efficiences drop off precipitously.)

The transmission output shaft is coupled to the propeller shaft, which must be held in precise alignment with water-lubricated grooved rubber bearings. Each of those bearings absorbs from 1 to 1.5 percent of the energy in the shaft. Obviously, the number, placement, alignment, length, and fit of those bearings must be very carefully considered.

And to the propeller. Propellers lose efficiency in a number of ways. They rarely rotate in an untroubled stream of water. The flow to a propeller is invariably turbulent because of the shaft and the strut that supports the shaft. Often there is a skeg or keel in front of the propeller which all but destroys the flow to much of the propeller's circle. If the prop is too close to the boat's hull, water compresses at the area nearest the hull and causes resistance. If the vessel's rudder has been positioned too close behind the propeller there will be a resistance-causing interference. Sterndrives and outboards have a big hub forward of the prop, encasing a set of bevel gears bringing shaft rotation from the vertical to the horizontal. And the prop itself is rarely perfect. It has been ground to compromise dimensions because it must operate from 0 to 4,000 rpm's—or even faster.

But because American boaters are hooked on speed, the designed point of optimum efficiency is a very narrow band at the uppermost speed ranges—even though, as we now know, little of the boater's time will be spent there.

Large-diameter, slow-turning (under 2,000 rpm) propellers are known to be the most efficient, but most propellers are small, and turn much faster than 2,000 rpm. Powerboaters don't like big propellers that stick down into the water too far. Prop hubs are short, and so blades must be narrow to avoid interfering with each other during high-speed rotation. Therefore, propeller frontal area is nowhere near an optimum 100 percent driving area. When the tips of the propeller blades are moving faster than 120 mph, most propellers will cavitate—vaporizing the water they pass through—and large bubbles of gas that appear all over the blades cause them to lose thrust. Tip vortices spill the thrust off the fastest-moving part of the blade, and hub interference affects the bottom third of the blade. A short section, from the leading edge to the thickest part of the blade, only about one-third of the way along the blade, possesses laminar flow and is thus working hard. Transitional and turbulent separated flow dissipates the thrust of the trailing (two-thirds) portion. It's a miracle they work at all.

Clearly there is a *lot* of room for improvement in propeller design. But here, as in so many other areas covered by this book, the boating industry has thought itself into a corner. It has surrounded itself with inviolable sacred cows that block every avenue of investigation other than the most conservative levels of refinement. The list of self-defeating litanies can only be summarized here:

"Propellers can't be bigger because then they'll be too deep." "They can't turn slower because then they'll have to be bigger." "They can't turn slower because boats absolutely must go as fast as possible." "They can't be made of plastic because they just have to be made of metal." "And fancy propellers are too expensive." "They can't run through variable-speed transmissions because—well—it just isn't done." "They can't counterrotate on the same shaft because that's too expensive and no one will buy them." "They can't look weird because no one will buy them." And on and on.

But this enormous loophole through which all our energy is escaping *can be closed,* and the closing won't require billions of dollars in research. Just look at the fundamentals.

Fact: Larger propellers grip the water much better than smaller ones.

Fact: Slow-turning propellers don't cavitate, and have much better flow patterns for increased thrust-per-rpm.

Fact: Tip vortices are controllable—and much more so at slower tip speeds.

Fact: Research into flow-straightening devices by the commercial shipping industry has identified four features which combine to increase vessel efficiency by over 15 percent: wake-equalizing ducts, asymmetrical aftbodies, Grothues spoilers, and vane wheels. In addition to those features, commercial shipowners have pushed efficiency gains well beyond 20 percent through the use of very large propellers, which have skewed blades much like the new generation of smooth-running, fuel-efficient turbofan aircraft propellers under development today,* and submarine propellers. All of these exotic-sounding features have pleasure boat applications.

Fact: High-speed propellers will cavitate. Therefore, supercavitating (meat-cleaver) propellers, currently found only in surface-piercing drives and ultra-high-performance sterndrives, can be expected, with some modification, to run efficiently underwater in more conventional applications. If cavitation doesn't provide enough gas to fill the void behind those propellers' fat trailing edges, then introduce some air.

Fact: Large-diameter five- and six-blade propellers, operating at below 2,000 rpm, with skewed blades and tip vortex control, would operate on a longer hub with improved efficiency.

Fact: Variable-pitch propellers (operator or electronically controllable) operate at constant speed and adjust their pitch (by changing blade angle) for best efficiency at different speeds. This eliminates the need for a heavy transmission, since the pitch can be set all the way into reverse, but most important can allow a cruising motorboat to be "tuned" for best operating efficiency, lowest engine rpm's, and fewest emissions. Variable-pitch propellers have been an indispensable feature of aviation for over fifty years, and are well known in the marine markets of northern Europe. As one might expect, however, they fall outside that intangible range

* Blaurock, 1990; Paetow, 1991.

of acceptable normalcy that the American boating public is so docilely trained to accept, and have found little market share here. They are not yet small enough to be suitable for outboard motors.

What Works

I think that it is now time to present some conclusions about workable ideal power systems before moving into the powering of different boat types. Many possibilities have been considered, and we will be better equipped to identify vessels that meet our criteria if we separate the wheat from the chaff.

To repeat: our criteria for judging energy and engines were as follows.

1. Do they utilize renewable resources?
2. Do they maintain lowest emissions and lowest toxicity possible?
3. Do they maintain highest levels of efficiency?
4. Are they highly reliable?
5. Are they reasonable in cost?
6. Do they offer the greatest degree of adaptability and practicability?

While it is good to keep an eye on the future, there can be no doubt that potential near-term solutions are most important to evaluate right now. One cannot urge a congressman to pass legislation based upon technologies that will not see the light of day for another five years. We must ask: What is available right now, today, to reduce the 420-million-gallon hydrocarbon hemorrhage flowing from the tail pipes of pleasure boats all over the United States? What is feasible, technologically and financially, today? And what can reasonably be "forced" in the near future?

First, and most critical, the two-cycle outboard must be so heavily discouraged by society that it all but vanishes from sight. It alone accounts for the vast majority of emissions from pleasure boats. We cannot consider the current generation of two-stroke engines as a viable source of marine power under any conditions.

But the outboard configuration itself need not be condemned. Alternative outboards need to be developed and distributed. One manufacturer (Honda) already makes a growing line of competitive clean-burning four-cycle outboard motors. Any of the outboard motor manufacturers could convert to building four-cycle engines if circumstances warranted.

Next, fit those four-stroke outboards with catalytic converters. The converters can be air-cooled external add-ons, with pop-up buttons indicating when backpressure has exceeded optimum. The catalyst can be unscrewed, washed and air-blasted out, then replaced.

And if the Orbital / EBDI two-strokes do materialize, so much the better.

Second, all inboard and sterndrive engines, whether spark-ignited or compression-ignited, can be outfitted with fuel injection (diesels already are), turbochargers, EMS, exhaust aftertreatment, and all the sophisticated internal design features that contribute to clean burning. Engines can be smaller and lighter for the same power output.

If dry exhaust is workable from an engineering point of view, as I believe it to be, then automotive engines of almost any stripe can be readily adapted to marine use, outfitted with exhaust aftertreatment, and installed in most boats. Automotive engines carry with them the added benefit of widespread parts and repair networks, and lower unit costs because they won't have to undergo expensive, low-volume "marinizing," which consists primarily of wet-exhaust castings.

Third, despite a number of environmentalists who have

all but written the epitaph of the diesel engine, I've concluded that diesels have the potential to become the single best clean-power engine of choice. Very soon the combined effects of improved combustion through internal refinements, turbocharging, and EMS, reduced sulfate emissions from reformulated diesel fuels or alternate fuels, and very significant particulate and NOx reductions from two- or three-way exhaust aftertreatment, all acting upon a motor that is already a low CO and CO_2 producer and a fuel-efficient thermal converter, will yield a power package that should deliver very-low-emission high-torque marine performance for years to come.

Fourth, when the application does not absolutely demand high speeds, a combination of internal combustion generator with a large bank of storage batteries and electric propulsion motors, called "hybrid" propulsion, has the capacity to dramatically reduce emissions and still provide a moderate amount of power with long cruising ranges. Such a system also offers less tangible benefits, such as silent or near-silent operation and very low fuel costs. Battery upgrades as new technologies come to market will improve performance.

Fifth, battery power alone, rechargeable from shore power, produces no emissions and is very suitable for local recreational and utility boating. Electric propulsion has a track record of very low maintenance and "fuel" costs. Periodic battery upgrades, again, will profoundly improve performance.

Powerboaters can be (and I know that many are already) programmed to enjoy boating at 15 knots instead of 30. Better still, 5 knots instead of 50.

Put yourself aboard a boat going 50 knots. The only part of the brain that can still function, beyond the part that controls survival, is the part that controls ego. The ego is on the wing, soaring, John Wayne in his character Rusty, against all the odds attacking the enemy cruiser with Lt. Bulkeley in the Philippines. But at 5 knots the world changes. You see and hear everything. You carry on a conversation. Can that be too radical?

Most marinas already have facilities suitable for charging the battery banks of electric and hybrid boats. Additional facilities can be built if electric propulsion becomes widespread. Any electrician can handle the job; there is nothing unusual about it.

Sixth, local utilities can work with marinas to install natural gas filling facilities at marinas. The reduced likelihood of oil spills should help ease permitting and reduce insurance rates.

Seventh, spark-ignition engines can be converted from monofuel to multifuel, using the "exotic" fuel (CNG, methanol, ethanol, etc.) for local trips. Rental fleets and municipal fleets can readily be converted to multifuel use.

Eighth, propellers can be made much, much better, especially if boaters can be convinced to live with slightly deeper draft. Sailors have no problem with a small boat that draws two feet, and a bigger boat that draws four. Powerboaters can adapt too. Variable-pitch propellers and variable-ratio transmissions can be successfully fitted to many types of boats, with real benefits.

And there it is. An eight-point repowering plan. Now, with a respectful nod toward the future, toward hydrogen, methanol, fuel cells, ultra-low-emission two-cycle engines, and batteries with 250 watts per pound of energy densities, we must look at what we can achieve with boat design today.

We have identified clean sources of energy and clean propulsion systems, but it is not enough to rely on that knowledge alone. *The boat itself must match the power,* otherwise we are wasting our time. We must develop boat forms that do not have high resistance characteristics, and that do not require of an engine the unremittingly high torque loadings that will defeat any efforts to reduce fuel consumption and clean up the exhaust.

Good energy, clean power, and *low-resistance boats.*

6

———◆———

Low-Resistance Boats

Two Fluids and an Interface

IN THE LATE 1970s, when American automakers finally faced the realities of ever-more-stringent emission and fuel mileage standards, they were forced to examine every possible resource available to them for solutions. Some of those resources we have already discussed. But clean engines and catalytic converters would be only half as effective as they are without the profound reductions in resistance—rolling drag and aerodynamic drag—that automakers achieved through focused redesign of the entire automotive "platform."

Today automobiles, and increasingly trucks and buses, exhibit carefully sculpted rounded lines and smoother bodies, with flush-fitted windows, gutters, and handles. These changes have not been made solely to gain a new, fresh "look," as many think, but to enable a program of across-the-board motor downsizing that will help meet some very hard-nosed emission standards. Underneath the body panels there are lighter, but stronger, frame structures. For the same reason that it is easier to pick up and carry a lighter object than a heavier one, the lighter cars need less energy to accelerate, climb hills, and maintain highway speeds.

The same changes will have to be made in boats—but the challenge will be greater. Unlike cars, which are immersed in a single low-viscosity fluid (air), boats operate in three media simultaneously: the fluid called air, the fluid called water, and the interface where the two meet. Each medium has its own set of unique friction and flow characteristics, but the interface adds a third, and much less predictable, component of resistance: the wave.

At once cradle and mortal enemy, the wave constrains a boat's every attempt at graceful movement, pummeling and pounding, dragging at its heels like quicksand. The wave poses a design challenge that has puzzled engineers for centuries.

One Log or Two?

There is no single perfect boat. In fact, there is nothing that could even truly be called a normal boat. A standard boat. Since the first anthropoid straddled a log on the shores of Lake Victoria to reach a dead deer that had expired just beyond his reach, humankind has been "improving" waterborne transportation without respite. The next hunter lashed two logs together, and was able to paddle farther than the first. Since then, every sailor, every builder, every designer, rigger, mechanic, painter, every boatyard floor sweeper has had his influence upon the next boat to go down the ways. Boats seem to bring out the artist / engineer in everyone.

This ceaseless fiddling has taken boat design down a number of blind alleys. We have encountered a few of them in these pages. One path, however, has remained straight, true, and consistent: the quest for a seaworthy, easily driven hull. All the great explorations and migrations of humankind, and most of the great civilizations, have followed and depended upon the development of a superior watercraft. The low-resistance boat.

The earliest known ocean voyagers were the forebears of the Polynesians. Long before European watermen dared sail out of sight of land, before the great pyramids were built, a race of seafarers left islands in eastern Indonesia and the Philippines to venture into the western Pacific. By the time Europeans, in the person of Captain James Cook, "discovered" Hawaii in 1778, while the American Revolution was just getting under way and Adam Smith was celebrating the publication of his *The Wealth of Nations*, those islands were the home of a seafaring people that had been comfortably ensconced for 2,000 years.

Their vessels, hollowed logs lashed to crossbeams with rope and powered by strange crab-claw—shaped sails, seemed primitive to the European adventurers, hardly likely to be seaworthy. And yet Cook's journals report that the native craft could outsail and outpoint any of his ships' boats, and the mother ship as well, and that long reaches of open ocean were being regularly traversed by those odd craft without benefit of compass, chart, or clock.

Three centuries earlier, Portuguese regent Henry the Navigator had sponsored development of the first true off-shore-capable ship—evolved from thousands of years of coastal voyaging vessels—and of navigation techniques that would allow sailors to proceed and return with scientific (repeatable) precision. Had Columbus tried to reach the Indies forty or fifty years earlier than he did, he might indeed have fallen off the end of the world—there were no European vessels suitable for transoceanic exploration.

If one were to trace all the world's ships and boats back through time to a common "Eve," it would probably be that log on the banks of Lake Victoria. Subsequent development would show as a bifurcation: some civilizations persisted over thousands of years in trying to improve the tippy single log while others just lashed two logs to some poles and went sailing. Ironically, the civilizations that stubbornly, plank by plank, rivet by rivet, metamorphosed the single-log vessel into today's supertankers triumphed, in the long run, over the peoples who, with prescient engineering acumen, achieved transoceanic capability thousands of years earlier with the double-log vessel.

Multihulls

As Cook noted, the double-log canoe, or catamaran, was faster than the portly European monohulls. The hulls of the Polynesian catamarans and proas were proportioned long and thin, whereas Cook's boats (and indeed the mother ship as well) were short, fat, and heavy. While there might have been little difference in the number of men required to paddle each type of craft at speeds of 2 or 3 knots, Cook's men would soon have been winded, panting and collapsing on the thwarts from the effort of rowing 4 knots. The Hawaiian boat, however, would soon have been hull-down on the horizon, leaving nothing but a pair of thin swirling wake lines to mark its impudent passage.

Of all the boat types we can attempt to match with our new clean propulsion systems, perhaps none has as much immediate potential as the *multihull*, a direct descendant of Polynesian voyaging craft. How did the Hawaiian multihulls outrun Cook so easily?

Multihulls are fast because they adhere, over a broad range of speeds, to the most fundamental rule of hydro (and aero) dynamics: *Lose as little energy as possible to the medium you are passing through.*

The entire science of resistance can be reduced to the behavior of a single molecule. Visualize one molecule of water with a boat headed straight toward it. The distance that tiny particle will have to be pushed aside and pulled forward by the passing of the boat, and the character of its motion (even or abrupt) as the boat goes by, determine the resistance of the boat. If the molecule is pushed aside only slightly, and the motion is gradual, the boat is expending less energy pushing water aside than a different hull that might cause the molecule to move more suddenly over a greater distance. Abrupt motion, caused by non-stream-lined obstructions to flow, disturbs a greater area of the out-lying fluid than the easy motion imparted to a fluid that is being gradually and evenly parted. The same applies to air molecules.

It's not really as simple as that, of course, because of the endless variations of boat types that we must briefly examine—displacement, semi-planing, planing, stepped planing, penetrating (which includes multihulls), semi-submersible, foil-borne, and hovercraft. Each of these creates a new set of variants on those simplified conditions. Still, the behavior of that one molecule remains the key to evaluating and understanding resistance.

A multihull, which distributes its lesser weight evenly over a long, cigar-shaped hull, will move the molecule much less, and much more gradually, than a conventional hull. At any given point along the boat's passage through the water it is only displacing, or pushing aside, a small fraction of what the conventional hull would. An astute observer with an engineering mind will notice, however, that it shouldn't matter whether the same amount of energy is expended all at once (conventional hull) or over a longer period of passage (multihull). In a single fluid, within the rules governing clean flow, the observer might have a case, but the actions of most boats are not taking place in a single fluid. They are disruptions of the surface tension at the interface of two very dissimilar fluids.

As we have seen, the factor that constrains speed and behavior of boats is the wave. And multihull boats, which belong to the family of *penetrating* hulls, cheat the wave.

Because they are not asking too much water to move aside at any given point of their passage, they exhibit greatly diminished wavemaking. Water simply mounds up beside the boat as it passes, stays there, and then falls into the hull's trough as the transom goes by, thereby circumventing the dynamics of wave forming. To a lesser, but still very real, extent, the flow characteristics around a long, thin transom-sterned monohull will be similar. Many penetrating power cruisers of the 1920s and 1930s achieved levels of efficiency that have not been seen since despite all the new technology that is available.

Displacement Hulls

Waves are a function of the interface. They are formed in reaction to the conflicting forces at play within two adjoining fluids of very different densities. The conventional European hull, as rowed by Captain Cook's stalwart crew, makes a deep hole in the water when it passes, and the water that was pushed aside follows the boat inexorably, trying to fill the hole back in. That wave is called the quarter, or stern wave, and it is the product of a hydrodynamic suction that full-bodied boats, called *displacement* hulls, cannot escape, no matter how much power is applied.

At the upper end of such a boat's speed range enormous amounts of energy can be wasted by an overzealous skipper thinking that his boat is going faster. The boat will squat and try to climb the backside of its own bow wave, it will root (steer erratically), roar, and vibrate—but the bow and stern waves will just grow larger and larger, and the boat will remain in the same attitude, at the same speed. Period.

As noted earlier (see page 88), the average limiting speed of a displacement hull is expressed mathematically as 1.34 $\sqrt{\mathrm{LWL}}$ (some short, heavy boats will be slightly slower, and some narrow, lighter boats will be slightly faster). Thus, if a boat is 36 feet long at its loaded waterline its top speed will be close to 6×1.34, or 8 knots. Approaching that speed, the boat's curve of efficiency will begin to fall like a stone as more and more energy is expended simply building huge and useless waves. Such a hull can, however, operate very, very efficiently if the panting operator will just back the throttles off a little, down to, say, $1.1\sqrt{\text{LWL}}$ —more efficiently, mile for mile, than any other type of boat, and with very little sensitivity to weight. At low speeds, wavemaking is greatly subdued and ceases to be a major component of resistance.

Sailboats, trawler yachts, offshore commercial fishing boats, classic launches, tugboats, rowboats, and all large ships fall into the category of displacement hulls. Improvements in displacement hulls, when they occur, tend to center around skin friction: reduced wetted surface, lighter structural weight, and improved flow across the bottom, its appendages, and its protective coatings. Wave resistance cannot be overcome. It is just a fact of life.

The displacement hull is invariably chosen for use when speed is not an issue, but when long range, great economy, and seaworthiness are vital. Eighty gallons of diesel fuel in a 30-foot launch I designed to cruise at $V = 1.2\sqrt{\text{LWL}}$ on 5 of its 18 installed engine horsepower could take that boat 1,800 miles. Eighty gallons of fuel? That's barely enough for a few hours of running and less than 100 miles of range in most of the 30-footers afloat today. Efficiency is achieved, therefore, through the combined influences of hull form (long and thin), selection of appropriate power (as little as possible), and user habits (less greed for speed).

Sailboats, depending on their relative sail area, are generally rigged ("powered") to reach hull speed in 10–12 knots of wind. Their performance is weighted toward the lower end of the Beaufort scale because on an average summer day (when the vast majority of sailboats are used) winds are likely to be light. A husky sea boat, built to take hurricanes at sea, will be just approaching hull speed in winds of 15–20 knots, whereas a purpose-built racer will lose races unless it is able to sail fast in the faintest cat's paw.

In any case, when the strength of the wind exceeds that needed to move the boat at hull speed, the remaining energy goes into wavemaking and heeling or pitching forces. Thus, in strong winds, a boat that is heeling over, rail awash, foaming along with all gear straining, *will actually go faster if the skipper gives the order to reduce sail.* The boat will then stand up straighter, exposing its sail plan at a more advantageous angle, and its keel will be extending deeper into the water, thereby helping the boat "foot" better. Many sailboat skippers know this, but the notion of less-is-more has yet to gain much acceptance among powerboaters.

Semi-Planing Hulls

A displacement hull is shaped underwater like an avocado that has been cut in half: the front is somewhat narrowed, the midsection is full-bodied, and the aft end slopes back up toward the surface. When the midsection is made less full, however, and some of that buoyancy can be shifted to the aft end, the boat's underwater flow lines run flatter and the hull starts to develop lift. That lift dissipates wavemaking somewhat, and allows the boat to physically rise in the water as it runs.

The resistances acting upon such *semi-planing* hulls are more complex, and are composed of wetted surface friction, appendage drag (from struts, shafts, rudders, through-hull fittings), a reduced amount of wavemaking, and the drag component of lift (lift always creates drag—ask any aircraft designer—and minimizing drag while maximizing lift will therefore be a critical aspect of any lifting design). Semi-planing hulls, despite being subject to a new form of drag, benefit in terms of absolute speed from the lift they can develop and are able to exceed their theoretical hull speed. They are capable of operating at speeds ranging from $V/\sqrt{\text{LWL}} = 1.8$ to $V/\sqrt{\text{LWL}} = 2.5$, although they need an exponential increase in horsepower to do so.

Flying on Water:
Part I—Planing Hulls

As speeds increase through and beyond that range a vessel is said to be a *planing* hull. It must possess an afterbody that is virtually prismatic in shape to all but eliminate the suction that is still present in semi-planing types. As the boat runs, a concentration of lifting forces gathers under the center of gravity, the boat naturally rises forward into an angle of attack, and then skims on top of the water rather than plowing through it. Wavemaking becomes a negligible source of drag; however, with an increase in the speed of water flow across the bottom, friction plays an increasingly important role.

With an increase in lift comes an increase in drag as well. Imagine the energy required to hold up a boat that weighs thousands of pounds. Propulsive thrust from the propeller is converted to that lifting force through the vector of an inclined plane—the boat's bottom.

Planing hulls today are capable of routinely exceeding speed–length ratios of $V/\sqrt{\text{LWL}} = 10$ (a 20-foot boat going 45 miles per hour). Is there a gain in efficiency as the now-vestigial quarter wave is left farther and farther astern? Or does the power consumption required to overcome resistance and achieve lift defeat any possible gains? We will soon see.

There have been several successful, if eclectic, variants on the theme of planing. The basic quest has been for higher speeds and technological purity, but as speed is a measure of efficiency, there is something to be learned from these more exotic craft.

Very early in the development of planing hulls designers looked for ways to reduce wetted surface at high speeds. One of the first concepts they tried was the *stepped hydroplane*. In these boats the bottom was segmented into two or more inclined planes (the steps) arrayed transversely the full width of the vessel's bottom, creating an impression of steps or shingles (as indeed they were often called). The first stepped hull was sketched by one Reverend Ramus in 1872, and despite a few failures, stepped boats virtually ruled powerboat racing from 1906 until the advent of the three-point hydroplane in 1940, a type which still reigns supreme on the racecourse but has found no application in the pleasure boat market.*

Today stepped hydroplanes are still considered to be a fringe technology. Offering a stepped boat requires of the builder a commitment to a potentially expensive program of development activity: many modifications to the prototype, and possibly more than one prototype. Few builders are eager to embark on such a costly adventure, especially when so low a premium is placed on fuel economy and efficiency. The simplest solution, most builders conclude, is to stay with the product you know and stuff enough horsepower into it to get the speed you want. Even so, there are several builders offering stepped hydroplanes in their product lines, Wellcraft and Super Hawaii being two recognizable names among them.

Flying on Water:
Part II—Hydrofoils

The early days of experimentation with flight were avidly followed by boat enthusiasts. It wasn't long before boat

* Fostle, 1988.

designers began to think of underwater wings which would lift their boats completely free of the water, thus eliminating wetted surface friction and any vestiges of wave drag. Technological purity.

One of the most prominent tinkerers with *hydrofoil* technology was Alexander Graham Bell, world-renowned as the inventor of the telephone, who was sufficiently wealthy from his inventions to underwrite a major development effort. Starting in 1910, Bell and his collaborator, a young Canadian navy lieutenant named Casey Baldwin, built a series of hydrofoils that attained speeds of over 50 miles per hour in 1913 and a world-record 70 miles per hour by 1919.*

Despite a very promising beginning, hydrofoils have seen only limited application. Large amounts of power are required to lift the entire weight of a vessel clear of the water. The foils are vulnerable to floating obstructions, and are efficient only over a narrow band of operating speeds. Rough sea conditions can limit the hydrofoil's ability to "fly," and when such a craft slows enough to handle heavy weather or maneuver in harbor, the immersed foils exert a tremendous drag.† Several types of foil-borne ships are still in use at this time, primarily as ferries and military patrol craft, each sporting foils best for the vessel's designed optimum speed, but the genre has undergone little new work in recent years because of disappointments resulting from high costs and logistical limitations, and can be considered moribund—a blind alley. Despite advantages such as low shock loadings and good comfort levels, hydrofoils did not prove to be any more efficient than less-expensive conventional craft.

There is one hydrofoil concept in development, however, that may be adaptable to recreational uses. Garry Hoyt of

* Mackenzie, 1928.
† Cagle, 1970.

Newport, Rhode Island, advertising-exec-turned-boat-builder-turned-designer, is experimenting with a small boat (using one of his less successful small sailboat hulls) that is fitted with a simple foil aft and a broad, deep-V ski forward. In a remarkable feat of intuitive design, Hoyt's craft performed enticingly well right out of the shop. It rides smoothly over large chop, banks correctly in turns, stays in trim despite changes in load, and reaches 25 miles per hour with a single 15-horsepower outboard motor.[*]

Flying on Water:
Part III—Hovercraft

Going the final step beyond hydrofoils are seagoing vehicles called *hovercraft* which lift themselves bodily out of the water and ride on a cushion of air. Early hovercraft were powered by propellers in the water, but most in service today are driven by airplane propellers. With no underwater appendages at all, hovercraft can move very fast, and they are able to run completely out of the water to dock or even travel some distance on land.

Several enormous hovercraft are in commercial service (similar to an airline) on the English Channel run, but repeated attempts to enter the pleasure boat market with small hovercraft have met with little success. Noise, cost, sea-state limitations, and other operational quirks have stalled hovercraft development. Hovercraft have not provided any gain in efficiency that might be viewed, from our perspective, as an incentive to promote further development.

[*] Hoyt, 1988.

Semi-Submersibles
and Wave-Piercers

Finally, in an attempt to escape the bonds of wave action on larger vessels, naval architects have conceived a hull form that suspends torpedo-like hulls beneath the water with a superstructure suspended atop them on tall, buoyant, streamlined legs. Called *SWATH*, these ships are an emerging type with good prospects. They belong to a conceptual genus called *wave-piercing*, in which resistance from pitching in head seas is reduced at the same time wave form drag is reduced.

Such hulls go through seas rather then leaping (sometimes violently) over them, and enjoy resistances more akin to those found affecting torpedoes or submarines, which are completely immersed and thus vulnerable only to skin friction, appendage drag, and shock waves similar to those produced by supersonic aircraft. Submarines and torpedoes, like fish, can travel at very high speeds with relatively low power output.

Logistics, again, limit the recreational applications of these vessels. Because a SWATH ship is suspended by a carefully monitored neutral buoyancy in its semi-submerged hulls, it will only respond to oncoming waves as a function of the very limited buoyancy available in the connecting structures that hold the superstructure aloft.

This characteristic gives it a comfortable ride, but severely limits its practicality in the smaller sizes commonly found among recreational vessels. A small recreational SWATH boat would have to stand absurdly high, with the concomitant windage, to stay out of an everyday chop, and would be prohibitively sensitive to changes in passenger loading.

Nevertheless, well-designed buoyant wave-piercing catamarans and trimarans, such as those under development by Roger Hatfield at Gold Coast Yachts, have a lot of potential for improving the comfort of a pleasure boat's ride while simultaneously reducing pitching-induced drag and wave form drag.

Defining the Efficiency of Boats

How do these diverse types compare with each other in terms of efficiency? How can we identify what is useful? And discard what is not?

To answer these questions we will need a way to measure the relative efficiency of very different boats. It must be a broad-brush formula that utilizes readily available data, and responds correctly to input regarding the key parameters that affect a boat's overall efficiency: horsepower, speed, weight, and fuel consumption. (There is no need to take any of the boat's dimensions or other characteristics into account because we are concerned only with an outward evaluation of relative performance *ex post facto.*)

The formula will have to give a lower (poorer) number to a boat that consumes more fuel, but must not penalize speed—in fact speed is a measure of efficiency if it is achieved sensibly. The formula must reward a boat that goes faster with less horsepower, it should reward hard work (a boat that is heavy but runs efficiently), and cannot be punitive toward sophisticated lightweight structures.

Therefore I submit the following formula as the simplest means of measuring efficiency. A higher number indicates better efficiency.

V = The boat's top speed.

gph = Gallons per hour of fuel consumed by all engines at top speed. If no observed data are available, use specific fuel consumption for similar engines—that is, 0.4 pound per horsepower-hour for diesel, 0.5 pound per horsepower-hour for gasoline, 0.6 pound per horsepower-hour for outboards. gph is constant with horsepower.

Δ = The boat's weight.

$$\frac{\left(\dfrac{\Delta}{\text{gph}}\right) \times V}{10^4} = \text{efficiency rating number.}$$

Let us see how the formula works. Weight divided by gallons per hour will reward low fuel consumption (and low horsepower, and therefore lower emissions), but will also award a higher, more favorable number to the harder-working heavier boat, encouraging strength and low cost. Multiplying the resulting product by the boat's maximum speed potential will reward speed, encouraging efficient aerodynamics, hydrodynamics, engines, and propeller design.

If, for example, a new propeller is developed, enabling a boat's speed to increase by several knots, the formula will reward it with a higher number. If the boatbuilder chooses to use the new propeller as a means of reducing horsepower, emissions, and fuel consumption, the formula will reward that choice instead. If the builder wishes to cut weight from his structure, the formula will cover him by rewarding his boat's resulting greater speed (V) or lower fuel consumption (gph). Dividing the equation's product by 10^4 (10,000) simply brings the numbers down to earth. They are more readily compared if they are smaller.

Please note that engine exhaust emissions are not yet a factor in the equation. For the sake of unbiased comparison it must be assumed that all engines emit equally as a function of their fuel consumption. At a later date, with the availability of precise emission data from boats, the formula can be amended to reward low emissions and discourage dirty engines.

To begin building a data base for the sake of comparison, let us apply the formula to some representative boats and assign them their efficiency ratings:

30-foot launch described above (18 hp): 11.7
45-foot trawler yacht (135 hp): 4.91

38-foot catamaran with 10-hp outboard auxiliary: 4.5
36-foot auxiliary sailboat (60 hp): 4.46
1929 Elco flattop 42-foot cruiser (160 hp): 3.36
53-foot 49-passenger day-cruising catamaran (90 hp): 3.14
40-foot power catamaran (360 hp): 2.16
36-foot lobsterboat, semi-planing (150 hp): 2.0
30-foot cruiser, planing (520 hp): 1.16
30-foot offshore deep-V muscleboat (800 hp): 0.82
18-foot sterndrive runabout (160 hp): 0.81
24-foot inboard runabout (300 hp): 0.79
18-foot runabout with 150-hp outboard: 0.78
20-foot pontoon boat with 60-hp outboard: 0.71

As I have indicated, the low-speed displacement hull wins all efficiency honors hands-down, despite wave form drag. Even a wallowing 36,000-pound trawler yacht is more efficient than most pleasure boats. The silver medal goes to penetrating hulls like the long, skinny Elco cruisers of a half-century ago, and a variety of multihulls. The bronze is awarded to semi-planing boats, whose hull form is a mixture of displacement and planing characteristics.

And finishing dead last is an array of boats that the industry has been force-feeding us for the last thirty years: overpowered and wasteful runabouts, cruisers, and the current best-selling "aluminum products" (the industry's term for watercraft built of aluminum, such as pontoon boats). It would seem, therefore, that the gains attributable to the advent of planing hulls are more than negated by the burden of power required to get on top of the water. The wave cannot be deceived.

Displacement-hull boats, occupying three of the top four rankings, are clearly going to be the first choice where the environment is concerned. By any measure of efficiency, they are far superior to other types. With small motors and large, slow-turning propellers they consume much less fuel and convert it much more efficiently into useful work. Since they have smaller motors and consume less fuel, emissions are less of a problem to start with, and are therefore easier to manage with the systems we discussed in the previous chapter.

Speed on the water is often, however, a practical necessity and an undeniable component of the pleasure in pleasure boating. Therefore displacement boats will not suit everyone. Working our way up the speed–length scale from $V/\sqrt{\text{LWL}} = 1.3$ we soon enter the domain of the penetrating monohull, like Elco's remarkably efficient sixty-year-old flattop, the semi-planing hull, and the multihull. Our preferred choices for nonpolluting watercraft are likely to come from these ranks. But what is the potential for mass-market applications of such boats?

Sensible Boating?

History is not encouraging. If common sense is to be the sole motivator behind a significant shift toward efficient watercraft, the shift may not occur at all.

The most articulate proponent of sensible boating is a Florida yacht designer named Tom Fexas, who coined the term "penetrating" which I have been using to describe long skinny boats that enjoy a low level of wave form drag. Ten years ago, at the New York Boat Show yacht design symposium, he read a paper entitled "The Elastic Trawler,"* describing the virtues of long-legged cruising boats that exchanged length for width and economy for profligacy. He sketched the specifications of a wonderful boat that met the demographic requirements of the average well-heeled weekend boating family. It was longer, narrower, and cost no more to own than a stubbier cruiser that couldn't range as far afield in the limited time available to the weekend voyagers.

* Fexas, 1982.

Fexas has had some success turning his theories into boats, and quite a few of his *Midnight Lace* cruisers have been built. They are very attractive boats modeled after the Elco cruisers of the 1930s and 1940s. The prototype for the series was 44 feet long and only about 12 feet wide, with over-hanging spray chines above the waterline that allowed the underbody to be narrower yet. The boat was not very exotically constructed, just moderately light in weight, and was powered only by a pair of 175-horsepower diesels—unheard-of for a boat that large. And yet she was able to go almost 30 miles per hour. How does our formula rate the original *Midnight Lace?* A very respectable 2.5.

Fexas's theory was based on an assumption that sensible boatowners, unwilling to spend ever-increasing hundreds of dollars for the fuel to take their weekend trips, would buy boats (presumably Fexas designs) that were more efficient. Unfortunately, the last decade has shown that boatowners will cheerfully spend hundreds, even thousands of dollars on a short cruise to sustain their illusions of speed and power. And Fexas, not one to let the world pass him by, has gone with the flow. He now draws enormous, wide, fuel-guzzling cruisers and sportfishermen (which rate in the area of 1.2 and below), and is doing quite well for himself. He is one of the very few household words in a profession that normally does not recognize or reward its innovators and stars.

Fortunately for the pleasure boat industry, a new crop of confident, idealistic tinkerers always appears, willing to risk millions of dollars on new ideas every year. Without them there would be virtually no development at all. But few of the new ideas seem to "take," and few of the entrepreneur / innovator / tinkerers survive more than a year or two. Despite the efforts of a small group of businessmen promoting electric boats, the ever-dwindling sailboat industry, and the trawler-and-tugboat crowd, the prognosis for a major auto-induced marine cleanup revolution is still very bleak.

Unless . . .

If there were suddenly to be an inescapable incentive for change—a California-style initiative, forcing the development of low-resistance, clean-power recreational boats—boatbuilders would find themselves panting to consider every option and look under every rock. The free market is wonderful that way.

The first place I'd suggest they look would be at the nascent potential of boats traveling at speeds from $V/\sqrt{\mathrm{LWL}} = 2$ to $V/\sqrt{\mathrm{LWL}} = 3+$, which would be, given that most pleasure boats fall between 18 and 30 feet in length, 10 to 20 miles per hour. What would such boats be like? And what other boats would builders be able to offer their public?

What Works

A lightweight 28-foot catamaran with acres of soft space on the trampoline between hulls could be outfitted with two 35-horsepower four-stroke outboards. This boat would be very seaworthy, easily converted via telescoping tube crossbeams into a trailerable or dockable width, and would move at speeds over 30 miles per hour. Rating: 1.3, a 65 percent gain in efficiency over today's sportboats, with ½₀th the emissions levels. Feasibility? Immediate. Add six months to develop an aftermarket catalytic converter bolt-on kit.

A 24-foot catamaran with two 20-horsepower electric motors and a battery bank in each hull. A tiny generator extends range and adds to speed. Solar panels can charge the batteries and extend range. Speeds approach 15 mph. Rating: 2.49. Feasibility? Immediate.

A 40-foot cruiser with every comfort of home and more. It is narrow, and the aft half of the bottom is shallow and flat for easy planing. The forward part of the bottom is rounded for a soft ride. Down the center of the bottom is a pod like the hull of a catamaran, part of the hull. It houses the weight of batteries where they are effective as ballast, and two 40-

horsepower electric motors spin skewed six-blade counter-rotating propellers on the same shaft. Inside the boat's tiny engine room sits a soundproof diesel generator of 30 kilowatts, to extend range and power. Top speed is 18 miles per hour, cruising speed is 12 mph, range is 500 miles. Rating: 5.4. Feasibility? Mostly immediate, but with one or two years of development time needed for the propellers and counter-rotating feature.

The same boat with 120 diesel horsepower. Rating: 5.1. Feasibility? Immediate. Add one to two years for particulate trap design and counterrotating feature.

A 30-foot open runabout, 7 feet wide. A single rotary (Wankel) engine of 175 horsepower, with dry exhaust and automotive catalytic converter, coupled to a Volvo duoprop counterrotating sterndrive, will consume 5 gallons of fuel per hour at an easy cruising speed of 18 mph. Top speed is over 30 miles per hour. Rating at cruising speed: 1.5. Feasibility? Immediate.

And if high speeds are absolutely essential, consider a *32-foot stepped planing sport cruiser,* needing only 400 horsepower to go over 35 miles per hour. Rating: 2.2—twice as efficient as conventional boats that do the same thing. With the exception of a particulate trap oxidizer, which will require one to two years of development and testing, such a vessel can be built tomorrow.

And what if high speeds are *not* absolutely essential? Can slow boating be as much fun as fast boating?

There are today hundreds of *electric boats* operating in the United States and a similar number in Great Britain, where a vast network of tiny, charming canals and majestic coastal rivers has created a market for slow, silent boats. Gliding through the hilly green pasturelands of southern England, a group of picnickers in an electric boat can literally hear the frogs and crickets on the banks of the canal.

Owners of electric boats wax rhapsodic about the virtues of their craft:

"You can't understand it until you've been out on one."

"It's not like any other boat you've been in."

"It's a whole new experience."

"I was out for four hours with some friends, and when I came back in my neighbors begged to go out. We went across the lake for dinner, and came home at nine o'clock. Then my daughter wanted to go out with her boyfriend. For the rest of the night, every time we thought about going in everybody would say, 'No, no, keep going.' We didn't go to bed till three A.M. when the batteries finally ran down."

"You won't believe it until you see it."

"We come in more relaxed than when we went out. That's never happened to us in a boat before. Usually with our last boats you'd come in all jangled up and happy to go inside and relax."

"I take clients out all the time. I can talk to them without shouting, in normal conversational tones. You can't even do that in most cars. Certainly not in a restaurant."

"My wife was terrified of the water. But somehow the boat felt secure to her. She knew it wouldn't go out of control or flip over, and it didn't make loud noises. Loud noise is a proven cause of anxiety. Did you know that?"

These comments are just a small sampling of remarks I have jotted down over the last several years. Some are so extravagant I couldn't include them here. The point I am making is simply this: there is, without any doubt, a strong potential market for boats that are quiet and slow. Electric propulsion can deliver such boats today, with operating times from 3 to 20 hours, at competitive pricing.

In the years to come, as battery technology improves, those same boats will be updated with new power packs, resulting in dramatically increased range or speed, and eventually both.

And the fundamental Achilles' heel of pleasure boating—the fact that no one really needs a boat—becomes everted to a positive element when one considers that because few people need to be out on the water in the first place, few boaters *must*, therefore, go specific speeds or distances in their boats. The market for boats is thus theoretically far more flexible and expansive than industry pundits would have us believe.

The dream of a boat in every driveway may finally be realized, ironically, through the advent of slow, silent craft that glide about the waterways amid a scattered chorus of distant conversation and laughter, and not, after all, because of the deafening exploits of a few wealthy raceboat drivers.

Marine Aerodynamics

To accomplish more with less. To move vehicles more efficiently with smaller motors, with as little sacrifice in performance as possible. To reduce engine exhaust emissions exponentially. The automobile industry has made remarkable progress toward those goals—proving that it can indeed be done—marching with the shotgun of government regulations at its back. Without reducing the rolling resistance of its vehicles, however, it would have had little success.

If today's auto showrooms were filled with cars that weighed and looked like 1965 Chevys, all the fancy engineering inside them would have been to no avail. Cars would groan away from the stoplight, take minutes to reach highway speeds, and then stay at those speeds only with the accelerator pressed to the floor. The rounded lines we admire on the road and in showrooms have not, therefore, been created solely on the basis of aesthetic considerations—although the appreciation of form does seem to follow function, and so we have come to like the sleek, organic shapes. The sculptured lines of cars have been designed by thin trails of smoke in the wind tunnel, and optimized by million-dollar computers, for the sole purpose of reducing the amount of energy required to move a body through a fluid medium.

Much attention has been given to the design and optimization of boat underbodies, and more will have to come, but none has been given to the other medium that boats travel through: air. To a man (and it is virtually 100 percent male), the industry's boatbuilders and designers are convinced that air resistance does not exert any significant influence upon boats. They are wrong. Without significant advances in the parallel development of *light weight* and *low aerodynamic drag*, which have become such essential components of aircraft and automotive engineering, pleasure boats will never achieve the gains in efficiency that are so urgently needed.

Designers will point with assurance at tables and charts of wind pressure coefficients, and these charts do seem to indicate that air resistance at speeds below 30 miles per hour is negligible. Among the host of other resistances that are currently standard operating procedure in the field of pleasure boat design—50 percent propeller losses, 20 percent engine efficiency, and poor hydrodynamic efficiency (friction, wave resistance, etc.)—air resistance may indeed be overlooked in the massive hemorrhage of horsepower.

But what happens when efficiency rises, when propeller losses are only 10 percent, hydrodynamic efficiency is excellent, and much less horsepower is needed? Aerodynamics assumes a new and critical role.

Wind pressure is calculated with the formula $P = 0.004V^2$ (V = wind velocity) per square foot of frontal area.* If a typical 32-foot power cruiser with 500–600 horsepower has a frontal area of 120 square feet, and is cruising at 25 miles per hour, then its air resistance will consume less than 20 horsepower, which is a very small percentage of the cruiser's overall wastage. This is as far as most designers go.

But what happens if the same boat is steaming into a headwind? Boats rarely operate in flat calm air. If that boat

* Kinney, 1973.

is encountering a 30-knot headwind, air resistance rises suddenly to 80 horsepower. And if the headwind is not precisely on the bow, but slightly off to one side, frontal area increases dramatically, and so does air resistance—*to as much as 30 percent of the total.*

Furthermore, when the cruiser encounters such a crosswind, it must alter its heading toward the wind to maintain course, much the way an airplane does, which creates a host of hydrodynamic problems. The vessel's rudders are going to have pressure on them constantly, which causes drag, and its entire underbody will now be presented to the water at an angle, with increased frontal area, diagonal flow lines, keel eddies, and increased appendage drag.

Small wonder, then, that the cruiser's skipper finds himself nudging the throttles forward again and again to maintain speed. He could be losing as much as 40 percent of his power to forces directly attributable to air resistance.

Powerboats are not, despite cherished beliefs to the contrary, subject to their own laws of physics. If they burn fuel, they pollute. And if the wind blows, they experience resistance just as any other vehicle does.

When a bicycle racer is straining to take his pull in a 32-mph breakaway, he is expending 88 percent of his energy overcoming wind resistance. Only 12 percent is left to overcome mechanical friction and gravity.

When a sailboat is close-hauled, sailing as high into the wind as it can, it gives up one-third of its available driving force to heeling, and of the remainder a further 50 percent, or more, is lost to the resultants of air resistance on hull and rigging before any power becomes available to drive the boat to windward.

A fit human being is capable of sustaining only 0.25–0.3 horsepower output. With careful design and a year of trials, this was enough to fly a man in the 200-pound *Gossamer Albatross* across the English Channel. A mere 6-knot headwind, however, almost doomed the trip as the time and effort to overcome the additional air resistance pushed pilot Bryan Allen to within seconds of his theoretical limits of physical endurance.*

To reduce the levels of pollution that emanate from powerboat tail pipes, air resistance will have to be minimized. The obvious way to accomplish that task will be to streamline. Eighty years have been spent in the wind tunnel researching aerodynamics in the field of aviation, more than thirty years in the field of automotive engineering, and zero years in the field of boat design (despite a few brief, isolated moments).

The entire concept of streamlining is analogous to one discovery that was made by airplane designers before the end of World War I: that a streamlined structural element (a wing or strut) exhibits far less drag than a comparable span of unstreamlined element. In fact, the airfoil wing of a well-built aircraft causes only the same amount of drag as a piece of wire one-tenth its frontal area. This led to a rapid abandonment of the wires that once braced biplane wings in favor of streamlined struts that could be stronger and larger with a lesser penalty in resistance.

Will we improve that 32-foot power cruiser if we reshape it with aerodynamic lines? Absolutely. First, it can be given a larger frontal area: more beam, more flare, a wider deck, and greater cabin volume. Second, it can be given less power—as much as 20 percent less—because of reduced wind resistance, with no penalty in cruising performance and safety. The benefits of reduced power are, of course, lower fuel consumption and fewer emissions. Third, it will exhibit reduced hydrodynamic resistance in crosswind conditions.

There are other compelling reasons to build aerodynamic boats:

* Grosser, 1981.

- An aerodynamic boat will lie to an anchor or mooring with much less strain on anchor and gear, and greater security.
- It will heave-to in violent squalls at sea with less difficulty, and better safety.
- Docking and close-quarters maneuvering will be easier because the unpredictable effect of crosswinds will be minimized.
- It will exert less strain on dock lines, cleats, and mooring hardware.
- The increased flare and wider topside form gives increased form stability for a safer, more comfortable boat.
- Strength and stiffness are inherent in rounded structures (the eggshell is an excellent example), so scantlings can be lighter, possibly less expensive.
- Aerodynamics melds with hydrodynamics in big seas, and an aerodynamic boat will shed and rise to big seas, losing less energy and thus increasing its safety factor, more easily than a vessel of conventional form. Big seas will be less likely to damage an aerodynamic boat than a more conventional one composed of flat panels.

Despite everything we have learned so far, there is no movement today at any level of the boating industry to improve pleasure boat efficiency and reduce emissions. There is only NMMA's wait-and-see attitude, and a complacent industry-wide technocentricity that makes it convenient to stubbornly maintain, based upon long-obsolete traditions and a single outdated (and possibly biased) report, that its products do not pollute. The industry has little incentive to change. Therefore nothing positive will happen unless concerned citizens force the issue. What can individuals do to overcome this inertia?

Fortunately, one need only follow the examples that have

been set by thousands of environmental activists over the last thirty years. Environmental activism is now an established, mainstream methodology. Dislodging corporate obstacles is nothing new. One should view the challenge not with trepidation, but as an excuse to have some good clean American fun.

Question authority. It's okay. Our country was founded on civil disobedience. Despite the political rhetoric of the American extreme right, lying down in front of bulldozers (or equivalent) is in the highest, most patriotic American traditions, tracing its roots directly to the American Revolution.

By now readers have undoubtedly formed opinions of their own about this matter. My questions, then, are:

- Do you agree that uncontrolled dumping of 56 million cubic feet of oil and hydrocarbons every year is a wildly excessive pollution allotment for *any* industry?
- Do you agree that the nationwide gross fuel consumption of pleasure boats is unjustifiable?
- Do you agree that most of the waste can be eliminated?

If so, what specific action should be taken next?

7

Take Back
the Waterways!

W E ARE FORTUNATE to live in a time when the needs of
the environment require little explanation, although
under the twelve years of conservative Republican presi-
dency they have been getting very little consideration. Writers such as Rachel Carson, Marston Bates, and N. J. Berrill
had to be part-scientist and part-poet to convey what was in
the late 1950s a radically new and unfamiliar message.

Today, however, environmental law is well established and
awareness is widespread. Ninety-two percent of us recognize the need for a clean and safe world, 52 percent are
openly sympathetic to environmental concerns, and 27 percent of us describe ourselves as active environmentalists.*

Still, when a new crisis unfolds, such as the one I have
outlined in these pages, there is no guarantee that any
remedial action will be taken. According to a study by the
Harvard Business School, the only thing that happens
"automatically" is the flow of foreign oil.† In today's polit-

---

* *Yachting*, 1992.
† Stobaugh and Yergin, 1983.

ical, social, and economic climate no gains will be made without a positive interaction among the forces of *government*, the *marine industry*, and the all-important dollar votes of the *consuming public*. To initiate action we must specify an agenda for each of the three categories.

But first we need a budget.

If we can agree—as the U.S. Department of Transportation did in 1982—that the most conservative estimates of the social cost (the money society spends to subsidize the burning of cheap fossil fuels: cleanup of tanker and barge spills, water treatment, acid rain damage to crops and food fish, treatment of skin and respiratory diseases, infrastructure deterioration, war, etc.) of one gallon of gasoline is $3, and pleasure boating burns approximately 2 billion gallons per year, then there is at the very least $6 billion in cash being wasted by society every year because of pleasure boating.

Next, let's say we are proposing to cut emissions 90 percent within five years, and that we choose to make 50 percent of the resulting savings immediately available to society as cash (by not spending it). We are left, then, with $2.7 billion as a theoretical annual budget for cleaning up the pleasure boat industry. If we anticipate losing half that amount to the political bargaining process, there will remain $1.35 billion dollars, which will be our theoretical budget. Our initiative can be designed to cost society nothing, not a penny, and it can in fact generate a positive cash flow for the nation. Further, the money spent will create thousands of jobs and a significant long-term benefit to society.

So, with the money theoretically in place, here are specific steps that must be taken within the next two or three years.

The Role of Government

1. Emission limits for pleasure boats similar to those applied to road vehicles must be established and mandated.

2. National goals and dates for compliance must be set, specifying the incrementally increasing proportion of clean-power products that must enter the marketplace.

3. Government must reestablish a system of tax credits, subsidies, guaranteed low-interest loans, and other incentives to reward use of nonpolluting technologies. Incentives are good business.

4. Ongoing water testing must be conducted to establish a body of knowledge that is sufficiently detailed to quantify the long-term discrete levels of hydrocarbon stressing on both air and water. The research is needed to discern between water problems and air problems, and to correctly apportion the resources that will be used to attack those problems.

5. Carbon-based waterway density limits must also be established. This will limit pollution stress on waterways by limiting emissions, not people.

6. State and federal agencies must discontinue the use of two-stroke outboard motors in their research fleets. They must be the first to set a positive example for the general public to avoid accusations of hypocrisy.

7. Tax credits should go to buyers of clean-power boats.*

8. Establish an incentive system of credits and / or subsidies for builders of clean-power boats and propulsion systems.

* Passell, 1992.

9. R&D expenditures in the field of clean power should be partially subsidized.

10. Marinas that install alternate fuel pumping facilities, including electrical charging stations, should be granted favorable tax status.

11. A marine industry branch should be established within the EPA, with a board of advisers composed of representatives from the boating industry, environmental community, and boaters. The staff would provide liaison, interpretation, and technical assistance to the marine industry and general public.

12. The tax burden on sales of alternate fuels should be reduced to encourage their adoption by boaters.

13. Producers of alternative fuels and energy should be granted subsidies, favorable tax status, and R&D grants.

14. Universities doing clean-power R&D should be helped. They are less expensive than corporate R&D departments.

15. Rental fleets using clean power should enjoy a tax credit and / or subsidy system to reward use of clean-power boats in fleets.

16. Buy-back incentives for outdated polluting boats and motors should be initiated. Based upon the Unocal program,* each "buy" is credited with preventing a specific amount of pollution. Programs like this could be run by corporations or local governments, or by manufacturers seeking to gain carbon credits.

17. And one small regulatory function: State governments should conduct vessel emissions inspections on an annual basis as they do with automobiles today. Fees or credits would then be based upon emission levels found at these inspections.

* Begley and Hager, 1992.

The Role of the Boating Industry

18. We must insist on a more positive attitude at NMMA. NMMA must pass formal resolutions calling for clean power.

19. An environmental liaison branch within NMMA would help builders and owners understand and interpret the new system. It should offer technical support for builders, owners, and marinas.

20. NMMA should conduct a public information campaign to promote clean power.

21. The boating industry must agree on a set of criteria to establish efficiency ratings for boats. Rating numbers will help customers evaluate boats prior to purchase, and will help marketing departments assess prospective sales impact. Ratings can also be the benchmark for incentive programs.

22. Boating magazines and trade publications must provide a forum for debate, innovation, research, and news about clean power.

23. New product warranties should specify maintenance that results in continued low emissions. Fuel / air mixtures must be kept in trim. Exhaust aftertreatment systems need periodic cleaning or replacement. EMS sensors and functions should be checked periodically and replaced preventively. Bottom cleaning and polishing is an important element of reduced resistance and should be renewed monthly. Propellers should be inspected for small nicks and dents that can inhibit their already submarginal efficiency. Most minor damage to propellers can be ground and polished out by hand. Engine cylinder compression checks should be conducted annually. Even slightly worn piston rings and cylinder walls can add 25 percent to hydrocarbon emissions. Warranty and maintenance programs like this should be

rated for performance by government, and can be one of
the criteria for determining levels of credit or subsidy allowance to manufacturers.

24. An active aftermarket for refitting existing boats should
be encouraged and rewarded. This would create thousands
of jobs in small, independent business.

25. Manufacturers should incorporate low emissions criteria into their maintenance schools, and consider licensing
free-lance mechanics as well, to maintain control over, and
credit for, the quality of maintenance work done on their
boats.

26. The industry must acknowledge excellence in the field
of clean power and design. NMMA, boating magazines, and
even individual manufacturers should establish prestigious
awards for achievement, innovation, and excellence in design,
craftsmanship, engineering, manufacturing, and many other
categories. Rewarding individual effort and character is the
soul of what America stands for.

27. The industry must put pressure on insurance companies, or consider self-insuring. Clean-power technologies,
which will feature statistically significant percentages of
nonflammable and low-flammability propulsion systems,
should in many cases entitle builders and boatowners to
significantly lowered insurance rates.

The Role of the Individual

28. Join one or more environmental groups, and restrict
your donations for exclusive use toward promoting clean
power in boats. Give generously, but earmark the money
for fighting emissions from powerboats. The group will then
be forced to apply your check to a restricted fund address-
ing the purposes you have specified, or refuse it altogether.

29. Form a local association of boaters and shore land-owners to adopt and act upon the position outlined in this book.

30. Convene a special meeting of your boat or yacht club to discuss and endorse the viewpoint of this book. And then go on record with your parent association and member associations. Notify your elected officials of the organization's stance.

31. Power follows the money route. Your purchasing habits speak much more eloquently than words. These "dollar votes" are the things businessmen watch as they decide what products to develop and offer for sale.

32. Tell the NMMA your next boat will have to feature clean power. Tell them you endorse the views in this book.

33. Tell boatbuilders that you will buy from them again only when they have incorporated clean power into their product line. Be willing to accept slower speeds, for the time being.

34. Place a premium on fuel economy in your own plea-sure boating. You are careful with expenses in most other aspects of your life. Is boating so different?

35. Insist that your environmental groups immediately halt usage of two-stroke outboards, and convert their research fleets to clean power.

36. Write or call your elected officials to tell them you endorse the views put forth in this book, and that you want to see the appropriate government initiatives introduced right now.

37. Write letters to the media endorsing the views set forth in this book. Politicians and environmental groups are sur-prisingly diligent about reading the op-ed and letters-to-

the-editor pages in local newspapers. Access cable TV can provide a local forum for concerned citizens.

38. Public meetings at all levels, from town board to state legislature, allow time for public comment. They need to hear from you. If you are nervous, bring a prepared statement and read it. Or ask to meet with your elected officials, petition in hand, in closed session.

Epilogue

———————

THERE MAY BE MUCH more to hydrocarbon pollution than meets the eye.

Unpredictable chemical "accidents" are beginning to happen on a global scale, with alarming consequences. Every time an element or compound foreign to the natural world is introduced in statistically significant quantities, the fundamental chemical stability of the ecosystem is threatened.

Sometimes the chemistry runs wild.

Acid Rain. Who could have predicted that sulfur dioxide from burning coal and nitrogen oxides from car and pleasure boat exhaust would combine with hydrocarbons to create rain with the acidity of lemon juice? Who could have anticipated that acid rain would aggressively destroy crops, forests, lakes and even erode churches, buildings, monuments—as if brazenly trying to erase the record of human civilization?

The Ozone Hole. Who could have imagined that whiffs of waste chlorofluorocarbons (like Freon) would travel with their chlorine atoms fifteen miles high into the pristine atmosphere, with results like Columbus's sailors bringing smallpox to the West Indian natives? Who could have predicted that each chlorine atom would separate oxygen atoms from up to 100,000 ozone molecules and threaten entire regions of the ozone that protects our planet from the sun's destructive high-energy ultraviolet radiation?

Smog. Did Henry Ford imagine, when he mass-produced the automobile, that hydrocarbons from unburnt fuel, lubricating oil, and evaporation would combine with oxides of nitrogen and sulfur in such quantities that a photochemical reaction would take place in sunlight, creating a caustic brown fog that would on bad days obscure the world from sight and bring the scourge of disease down upon innocent people? If anyone had tried to tell Ford that such a thing would happen, he would have suggested they take an extended vacation—to the sanatorium. But happen it has.

This chemical tinkering is getting to be a very high-stakes game. And nobody knows the rules. I have brought the subject up, here at the end of a book about oil and hydrocarbon pollution from boats, because I have a very bad feeling.

A bad feeling about *hydrocarbons*—and especially *chlorinated* hydrocarbons, the molecular chemistry that created DDT, Dieldrin, Aldrin, Chlordane, Heptachlor, and Endrin, the most aggressively poisonous substances on earth. Let me explain my concern, in the context of acid rain, smog, and ozone destruction:

Methane is a simple hydrocarbon molecule formed of four hydrogen atoms bound to one carbon atom. Chemists have discovered, however, that the hydrogen atoms can be replaced with chlorine atoms. Remove just one of the hydrogen atoms and substitute a chlorine atom in its place, and *methyl chloride* is produced. A carcinogenic industrial solvent.

Replace three hydrogen atoms with chlorine and the result is *chloroform*. A general anesthetic. Swap the fourth hydrogen atom for chlorine and *carbon tetrachloride* appears. Another carcinogenic solvent.

But methane is only a very simple hydrocarbon. Some of the materials we have encountered in these pages are fantastically complex, and endure in the oceans for years.

Molecular mutation of complex hydrocarbons with chlorine atoms could permeate the environment with lethal poisons more powerful than anything we have conceived in our worst nightmares.

Where will the chlorine come from? We have seen how a "harmless" compound—Freon—can cause problems on a global scale. Chlorine is far more common than Freon and all the chlorofluorocarbons combined. It is the active ingredient that purifies the water in millions of swimming pools and the municipal water systems of most cities in the world. Millions of tons of chlorine are manufactured annually. Some of it finds its way back to the oceans from which it was processed—stripped by electrolysis from sea salt, sodium chloride ($NaCL$), and transported as $C12$ in gas form for injection into water systems. Even phenols (simple hydrocarbons) that occur naturally in drinking water are found to link with chlorine atoms.

Several of the researchers whose work has contributed to this book reported finding quantities of DDT and other chlorinated hydrocarbons in seawater samples, even though those substances have been banned in the United States for over twenty years. Other scientists report that there is no airborne DDT to be found over the United States.

Cross et al.[*] found chlorinated hydrocarbon samplings highest in areas that also had the highest levels of regular (unchlorinated) hydrocarbons: urban areas, which would be the least likely to originate those predominantly agricul-

---

[*] Cross et al., 1987.

tural pesticides, unless through illegal manufacturing. "The high relative abundance of unweathered DDT," say the authors, "suggests recent input . . ."

Hardy et al.* found chlorinated hydrocarbons in 28 percent of their samplings in the Puget Sound area. Again, concentrations were highest in association with urban sites that exhibited the heaviest hydrocarbon samplings.

Where is it coming from?

We may be setting the stage, with man-made chlorine and man-made hydrocarbons, for another "unforeseen" global chemical event—the spontaneous reaction of chemical compounds in the natural environment to form deadly chlorinated hydrocarbons.

What if the event, a marine counterpart to the man-made events that inspired Rachel Carson's *Silent Spring,* is already taking place?

. . . most noticeable was [the ocean's] eerie lifelessness. I saw no birds, and no sea life . . .

The seas are almost empty of wildlife, and only idiots like us who sail the oceans seem to be noticing it.

There has been a massacre out there. The seas are turning to deserts.

* Hardy et al., 1987a, b.

Bibliography*

Alexander, C. P. "Gunning for the Greens," *Time*, February 3, 1992.

Allen, D. W., et al. *Effects on Commercial Fishing of Petroleum Development Off the Northeastern United States.* Woods Hole Oceanographic Institution, 1976.

Anonymous, "The Man Who Had Don Aronow Killed," *Motor Boating and Sailing*, July 1991.

Antonoff, M. "Science Newsfront: Fuel Cells Go on Line," *Popular Science*, October 1991.

AP (no byline). "Upstate Cities to See How Natural Gas Powers Buses," *Kingston Daily Freeman*, October 21, 1991(a).

AP (no byline). "Government, Big 3 Join in Electric Car Research," *Kingston Daily Freeman*, October 28, 1991(b).

Axiak, V., and J. J. George. *Bioenergetic Responses of the Marine Bivalve Venus Verrucosa on Long-Term Exposure to Petroleum Hydrocarbons.* Marine Environmental Research #23, 1987.

Barber, B. "Biomass for the Masses," *Omni*, May 1991.

Bates, M. *The Forest and the Sea.* New York: Vintage Books, 1960.

Begley, S., and M. Hager. "Adam Smith Turns Green," *Newsweek*, 1991.

Begley, S., and M. Hager. "Cold Cash for Old Clunkers," *Newsweek*, April 6, 1992.

Bergeson, L. *Wind Propulsion for Ships of the American Merchant*

---

* Included in this list are supporting materials that are not specifically cited within the text.

Marine. Washington, D.C.: U.S. Department of Commerce / MARAD Office of Maritime Technology, 1981.

Berrill, N. J. *The Living Tide.* Greenwich, CT: Premier Books, 1964.

Berthou, F., et al. *The Occurrence of Hydrocarbons and Histopathological Abnormalities in Oysters for Seven Years following the Wreck of the Amoco Cadiz in Brittany (France).* Marine Environmental Research #23, 1987.

Blaurock, J. "An Appraisal of Unconventional Aftbody Configurations and Propulsion Devices," *Marine Technology* magazine, SNAME, November 1990.

Boating Industry. The Boating Business 1991. Washington, D.C.: NMMA, National Sporting Goods Association, U.S. Department of Commerce, 1992.

Bob-Manuel, K. D. H., and R. J. Crookes. *The Use of Liquefied Petroleum Gas, Methanol, and Unleaded Gasoline in a Turbocharged Spark-Ignition Engine Operating on the Simulated ECE-15 Urban Cycle.* SAE Paper #900709, 1990.

Bose, N., and P. S. K. Lai. "Experimental Performance of a Trochoidal Propeller with High-Aspect-Ratio Blades," *Marine Technology,* July 1989.

Bray, M., and A. Pinheiro. *Herreshoff of Bristol.* Woodenboat Publications, 1990.

Broh, I., and Associates, Inc. *NMMA Boat Usage Survey.* Des Plaines, IL: IB&A, 1991.

Brooks, A. Presentation at the Northeast Sustainable Energy Association's Solar and Electric Vehicle Symposium, Manchester, NH, January 1991.

Brown, Peter W., Director of Research, Outboard Marine Corp., personal communication, 1990.

Brown, S. F. "The Theme Is Green: The Tokyo Motor Show," *Popular Science,* February 1992.

Brownlee, W. *"H.M.S. Warrior," Scientific American, 1988.*

Bryson, W. "The New World of Spain," *National Geographic,* April 1992.

Budney, P. A., and M. G. Andrew. *Flow-by Lead-Acid—Improving the Performance Standard for EV Battery Systems.* SAE Paper #900135, 1990.

Cadwalader, R. "Thermoplastics," *Professional Boatbuilder,* April / May 1991.

Cagle, M. W. *Flying Ships: Hovercraft and Hydrofoils.* New York: Dodd, Mead, 1970.

Caprio, D. "Two-Stroke Technology Advances," *Soundings,* September 1991.

Carson, R. *The Sea Around Us.* New York: Mentor Books, 1961.

Carson, R. *Silent Spring.* Boston: Houghton Mifflin, 1962.

Central Hudson. *Roseton Electric Generating Plant.* 1989. (A description of plant dimensions and specifications.)

Cheiky, M. C., and L. G. Danczyk. *Zinc-Air Powered Electric Vehicle Systems Integration Issues.* SAE Paper #910249, 1991.

Cheiky, M. C., et al. *Rechargeable Zinc-Air Batteries in Electric Vehicle Applications.* SAE Paper #901516, 1990.

Chmura, G. L., and N. W. Ross. *The Environmental Impacts of Marinas and Their Boats.* URI Marine Memorandum #45, 1978.

Clark, J. S. *The Oil Century.* Tulsa: University of Oklahoma Press, 1958.

Clark, R. W. *Edison: The Man Who Made the Future.* New York: G. P. Putnam's Sons, 1977.

Clarke, D. (ed.). *Anatomy of the Automobile.* London / New York: Galahad Books / Marshall Cavendish Ltd., 1984.

Clemans, J. "Volvo's Diesel Breakthrough," *Motor Boating and Sailing,* August 1991.

Coates, S. W., and G. G. Lassanske. *Measurement and Analysis of Gaseous Exhaust Emissions from Recreational and Small Commercial Marine Craft.* SAE Paper, May 29, 1990.

Cook, R. "Electric Car Showdown in Phoenix: Zinc-Air Battery Wins," *Popular Science,* July 1991.

Corcoran, E. "Cleaning Up Coal," *Scientific American,* May 1991.

Corner, N., et al. "Hydrocarbons in Marine Zooplankton and Fish." *Effects of Pollutants on Aquatic Organisms.* Cambridge, U.K.: Cambridge University Press, 1983.

Crook, W. *Power for the Small Boat.* New York: Dodd, Mead, 1947.

Cross, J. N., et al. *Contaminant Concentrations and Toxicity of Sea-Surface Microlayer Near Los Angeles, California.* Marine Environmental Research #23, 1987.

DEMI. *DEMI Technical Information: APS and SCE Zinc-Air Powered Honda CRX and the SOE Sponsored Zinc-Air Minivan.* Dreisbach Electromotive, May 14, 1991.

Dempster, N. M., et al. *The Composition of Gasoline Engine Hydrocarbon Emissions—An Evaluation of Catalyst and Fuel Effects.* SAE Paper #902074, 1990.

Dempster, N. M., and P. R. Shore. *An Investigation into the Production of Hydrocarbon Emissions from a Gasoline Engine Tested on Chemically Defined Fuels.* SAE Paper #900354, 1990.

Denny, S. B., et al. *A New Usable Propeller Series.* Marine Technology, Vol. 26, No. 3, 1989.

Desmond, K. *Power Boat: The Quest for Speed Over Water.* New York: Orion Books, 1988.

Dillingham, S. "Automakers Charging toward a New Battery," *Insight,* February 18, 1991.

DOE. *Annual Energy Review 1990.* Washington, D.C.: United States

Department of Energy, Energy Information Administration, 1991(a).

DOE. *Monthly Energy Review, August 1991*. Washington, D.C.: United States Department of Energy, Energy Information Administration, 1991(b).

Dostrovsky, I. "Chemical Fuels from the Sun," *Scientific American*, December 1991.

Downham, Don, Marine Motors Development, General Motors, personal communication, 1991.

Du Cane, P. *High Speed Small Craft*. Devon, U.K.: David & Charles, 1974.

Duncan, L. T. *Wind Tunnel and Track Testing an ARCA Race Car*. SAE Paper #901867, 1991.

Eberhard, G. A., et al. *Emissions and Fuel Economy Tests of a Methanol Bus with a 1988 DDC Engine*. SAE Paper #900342, 1990.

EPA. *Nonroad Engine and Vehicle Emission Study*, Report PB92-126960. Washington, D.C.: National Technical Information Service, U.S. Department of Commerce, 1991.

EPA / BIA. *Analysis of Pollution from Marine Engines and Effects on the Environment*, PB-242 175. Washington, D.C.: National Technical Information Service, U.S. Department of Commerce, 1975.

Essig, G., et al. *Diesel Engine Emissions Reduction—The Benefits of Low Oil Consumption Design*. SAE Paper #900591, 1990.

Fexas, T. "The Elastic Trawler," paper read at the Westlawn Yacht Design Symposium, January 23, 1982.

Fexas, T. "The Race for the Ultimate Sportfisherman" and "The Ideal Fexas Boat," *Professional Boatbuilder*, October / November 1989.

Flavin, C., and A. B. Durning. *Building on Success: The Age of Energy Efficiency*. Worldwatch Institute #82, 1988.

Flavin, C., and N. Lenssen. *Beyond the Petroleum Age: Designing a Solar Economy*. Worldwatch Institute #100, 1990.

Fleming, Joseph W., Jr., President, Electric Launch Co., Inc., personal communication, 1988–1990.

Fostle, D. W. *Speedboat*. United States Historical Society and Mystic Seaport Museum, 1988.

Fox, U. *Seamanlike Sense in Powercraft*. Chicago: Henry Regnery Company, 1968.

French, H. F. *Clearing the Air: A Global Agenda*. Worldwatch Paper #94, 1990.

Gallagher, J., et al. *The Colorado Oxygenated Fuels Program*. SAE Paper #900063, 1990.

Gardiner, W. W. "Sea Surface Films: Deposition and Toxicity in Intertidal Habitats," unpublished thesis, Western Washington University, 1992.

German, John, Project Director, EPA, personal communication, 1992.

Gladwin, T. *East Is a Big Bird.* Cambridge, MA: Harvard University Press, 1970.

GM. *General Motors and the Environment.* Communications and Marketing Department, General Motors, 1991(a).

GM. *1991 General Motors Public Interest Report.* May 15, 1991(b).

Goodman, B., and G. Cook. "Fueling the Future," *Solar Today,* March / April 1991.

Gordon, J. E. *Structures.* New York: Da Capo Press, 1978.

Gordon, J. E. *The New Science of Strong Materials.* Princeton, NJ: Princeton University Press, 1984.

Gould, Johnathan, Unique Mobility, Inc., personal communication, 1991.

Granholm, Lars, Director of Technical Services, NMMA, personal communication, 1992.

Grassy, J. "The Waste Oil Monster," *Garbage,* July / August 1991.

Green, G. "The Future According to Jim Randle," *Car,* December 1991.

Green, G., and P. Nunn. "Tokyo," *Car,* December 1991.

Greene, E. *Marine Composites.* Ship Structure Committee, U.S. Coast Guard, 1990.

Gribbins, J. "The Upstart Schooner that Started It All," *Nautical Quarterly,* #1, 1977.

Grosser, M. *Gossamer Odyssey: The Triumph of Human-Powered Flight.* Boston: Houghton Mifflin, 1981.

Hadler, J. B., et al. *Resistance Characteristics of a Systematic Series of Planing Hull Forms—Series 65.* SNAME paper presented May 9, 1974.

Hadler, J. B., and E. N. Hubble. *Prediction of the Power Performance of the Series 62 Planing Hull Forms.* SNAME paper presented November 11–12, 1971, New York.

Hamakawa, Y. "Photovoltaic Power," *Scientific American,* September 1990.

Hampson, George, Woods Hole Oceanographic Institute, personal communication, 1992.

Hanighen, F. C. *The Secret War.* New York: John Day Co., 1934.

Hardin, Jasper, Idaho National Engineering Laboratory, U.S. DOE, personal communication, 1990.

Hardy, J. T. "Where the Sea Meets the Sky," *Natural History,* May 1991.

Hardy, John T., personal communication, 1992.

Hardy, J. T., et al. *The Sea Surface Microlayer of Puget Sound. Part I: Toxic Effects on Fish Eggs and Larvae.* Marine Environmental Research #23, 1987(a).

Hardy, J. T., et al. *The Sea Surface Microlayer of Puget Sound. Part II: Concentrations of Contaminants and Relation to Toxicity.* Marine Environmental research #23, 1987(b).

Hayashi, K., et al. *Regeneration Capability of Wall-Flow Monolith Diesel Particulate Filter with Electric Heater.* SAE Paper #900603, 1990.

Hazelton, L. "Really Cool Cars: The Stakes Are High as Electric Cars Accelerate into the Showroom," *New York Times Magazine,* March 29, 1992.

Helmer, Earl, Chief Engineer, Yanmar USA, personal communication, 1992.

Henderson, R. H. *Philip L. Rhodes and His Yacht Designs.* Camden, ME: International Marine, Inc., 1981.

Hercules Engine Co. *Natural Gas Information Kit,* 1992.

Herreshoff, L. F. *The Common Sense of Yacht Design.* Jamaica, NY: Caravan-Maritime Books, 1975.

Hodgson, J. W., et al. *The University of Tennessee Methanol Corsica— Engineering for Low Emissions, High Performance.* SAE Paper #902100, 1990.

Hoffman, R. D. "The Peril of Leaking Tanks," *Popular Science,* March 1991.

Holt, D. J. "Tech Briefs" and "GM Sunrayce USA," *Automotive Engineering,* November 1990.

Holzman, D. "The Masterful Tinkering of Genius," *Insight,* June 25, 1990.

Honda. *Fuel Economy: BF 35/45 versus 2-Strokes, BF 35/45 Performance Curves; Fuel Consumption: BF 35/45 versus 2-Strokes;* and *Exhaust Emissions.* American Honda Motor Co., 1991.

Hounshell, D. A. *From the American System to Mass Production, 1800– 1932: The Development of Manufacturing Technology in the United States.* Baltimore: Johns Hopkins University Press, 1984.

Hoyt, G. *Ready About!* Camden, ME: International Marine Inc., 1986.

Hoyt, G., personal communication and videotape, 1988.

Hundleby, G. E., and J. R. Thomas. *Low-Emission Engines for Heavy-Duty Natural Gas-Powered Urban Vehicles—Development Experience.* SAE Paper #902068, 1990.

IEEE. "The Future of Power Generation," *IEEE* magazine, July/ August 1991(a).

IEEE. "Zinc-Air Battery Powers Best Car," *IEEE* magazine, July/ August 1991(b).

Itoh, N. "New Tricks for an Old Power Source," *IEEE Spectrum,* September 1990.

Janssen, P. A. "Sunrider's Odyssey," *Motor Boating and Sailing,* June 1991.

Jay, Benjamin E., ElectroSource International, Inc., personal communication, 1991.

Josephson, M. *Edison.* New York: McGraw-Hill, 1959.

Kataoka, T., et al. *Numerical Simulation of Road Vehicle Aerodynam-*

ics and Effect of Aerodynamic Devices. SAE Paper #910597, 1991.

King, R. J. "Solar Car Technology: A Revolution in American Design," *Solar Today*, March / April 1991.

Kinney, F. S. *Skene's Elements of Yacht Design.* New York: Dodd, Mead, 1973.

Kirby, B. "Designed to win," *Yachting*, supplement "America's Cup Challenge," 1991.

Kirschner, E. "Will the 21st Century Be Battery-Operated?" *Business Week*, December 24, 1990.

Kocan, R. M., et al. *Toxicity of Sea-Surface Microlayer: Effects of Hexane Extract on Baltic Herring and Atlantic Cod Embryos.* Marine Environmental Research #23, 1987.

Koelbel, J. G. *The Detail Design of Planing Hull Forms.* SNAME paper presented May 27, 1966.

Lapp, Steven, P. Engineer., Canada Ltd., personal communication, 1990.

Lean, Hinrichsen, and Markham. *Atlas of the Environment.* New York: World Wildlife Fund / Prentice Hall, 1990.

Lewandowski, Richard P., SunWize Energy Systems, Inc., personal communication, 1990–1991.

Linden, D. (ed.). *Handbook of Batteries and Fuel Cells.* New York: McGraw-Hill, 1984.

Lord, L. *Naval Architecture of Planing Hulls.* New York: Cornell Maritime Press, 1946.

Lowe, M. D. *Alternatives to the Automobile: Transport for Livable Cities.* Worldwatch Institute #98, 1990.

Machine Design. *Prototype Battery Boosts Electric Vehicle Range* (West Germany), *Machine Design*, July 26, 1990.

Mackenzie, C. *Alexander Graham Bell: The Man Who Contacted Space.* Boston: Houghton Mifflin, 1928.

Marchaj, C. A. *Aero-Hydrodynamics of Sailing.* New York: Dodd, Mead, 1979.

Margolin, R. "Rechargeable Batteries," *Powertechnics*, August 1989.

Mateucci, M. *History of the Motor Car.* New York: Crown Publishers, 1970.

McDonnell, M. "Last Gas," *Omni*, May 1991.

Meese, G. E. *Some Considerations in Power Cruiser Design.* SNAME, 1973.

Meyer, R. C. "Natural Gas Inspires Alternative Engine Design," SWRI, reprint from *Technology Today*, June 1991.

Meyer, R. C., et al. *Development of a CNG Engine.* SAE Paper #910881, 1991.

Miller, G. T., Jr. *Living in the Environment*, 7th ed. Belmont, CA: Wadsworth Publishing, 1992.

Milliken, A. S., and V. Lee. *Pollution Impacts from Recreational Boat-*

ing: A Bibliography and Summary Review. Rhode Island Sea Grant, 1988.

Modern Metals (no byline). "New Batteries Coming: None Uses Lead," July 1990.

Morgan, E. J., and R. H. Lincoln. *Duty Cycle for Recreational Marine Engines.* SAE Paper #901596, 1989.

Morris, D. "Making Fossils of Fossil Fuels," *Utne Reader,* May / June 1991.

Mother Earth News (no byline). "John Lorenzen: A Self-Taught Inventor," March / April 1980.

NAS. *Oil in the Sea.* National Academy Press, 1985.

Nelson, T. T. *A Hybrid Natural Gas Vehicle.* SAE Paper #901497, 1990.

Niesen, Jerry, Vice-President of Engineering, Mercruiser, Inc., personal communication, 1992.

Nixon, S. W., et al. *Ecology of Small Boat Marinas.* URI Marine Technical Report Series No. 5, 1973.

NMMA. *Inter / Port* newsletter, 1988–1991.

NMMA. *Boating 1991,* pamphlet of industry statistics, 1991.

Norton, J. A., and T. Elliott. "Current Practices and Future Trends in Marine Propeller Design and Manufacture," *Marine Technology,* Vol. 25, No. 2, 1988.

NSEA. *Symposium Abstracts* for December 1990 symposium at Manchester, NH; 5 papers.

O'Callaghan, R. A., et al. "The Aluminum-Air Reserve Battery—A Power Supply for Prolonged Emergencies," paper presented at the Eleventh International Telecommunications Energy Conference, October 15–18, 1989, Florence, Italy.

Paetow, K. A. "Ship of the Future," *Marine Technology,* July 1991.

Parish, C., et al. *Demonstration of Aluminum-Air Fuel Cells in a Road Vehicle,* SAE Paper #891690, 1989.

Passell, P. "Cheapest Protection of Nature May Lie in Taxes, Not Laws," *New York Times,* November 24, 1992.

Pattas, K., et al. *On-Road Experience with Trap Oxidiser Systems Installed on Urban Buses.* SAE Paper #900109, 1990.

Payne, P. R. *Design of High Speed Boats: Planing.* Fishergate, Inc., 1988.

Pelz, C. A., et al. *The Composition of Gasoline Engine Hydrocarbon Emissions—An Evaluation of Catalyst and Fuel Effects.* SAE Paper #902074, 1990.

Phillips-Birt, D. *Motor Yacht and Boat Design.* London: Adlard Coles Ltd., 1966.

Pickthall, B. "Are the Seas Turning to Deserts?" *Yachting,* August 1991, p. 28.

Pike, D. "Wind Can Have a Major Effect on Performance," *Work Boat World,* September 1990.

Pischinger, F., et al. *Modular Trap and Regeneration System for Buses, Trucks, and Other Applications.* SAE Paper #900325, 1990.

Ponting, C. "Historical Perspectives on Sustainable Development," *Environment*, November 1990.

Priebe, P. D. *Modern Commercial Sailing Ship Fundamentals.* Ithaca, NY: Cornell Maritime Press, 1986.

Raloff, J. "Dust to Dust: A Particularly Lethal Legacy," *Science News,* April 6, 1991.

Rawson, R. J., and E. C. Tupper. *Basic Ship Theory,* Vols. I and II. London: Longman Group Ltd., 1976.

Reece, N. S. "On the Road to an Alternative Fueled Future," *Solar Today,* March / April 1991.

Reisner, David, President, The Reisner Group, personal communication, 1990–1992.

Reisner, D. "A Sampling of Battery Options for Your Solar / EV Race Car," presented to NSEA Solar and Electric Vehicle Symposium, December 1990.

Reisner, D. "Batteries: It's a Jungle Out There!," presented at NSEA symposium, December 1991.

Reisner, M. *Cadillac Desert.* New York: Viking Press, 1987.

ReVelle, C., and P. ReVelle. *Sourcebook on the Environment: The Scientific Perspective.* Boston: Houghton Mifflin, 1974.

Ritchie, S., and D. Ritchie. "Zinc-Air EV Batteries," *Solar Mind,* May / June 1991.

Rod, James, Wildlife Biologist, Tidal Wetlands Ecology, personal communication, 1992.

Romano, S., and L. D. Price. *Installing a Fuel Cell in a Transit Bus.* SAE Paper #900178, 1990.

Rounds, George, Director of Association Services, NMMA, personal communication, 1992.

Rousmaniere, J. (ed.). *Desirable and Undesirable Characteristics of Offshore Yachts.* New York: W. W. Norton, 1987.

Rudavsky, S. "The Omni Energy Efficiency Guide: Saving for the Future," *Omni,* May 1991.

SAE. *Electric Vehicle Design and Development,* various papers and authors, SAE publication SP-862, 1991(a).

SAE. *Vehicle Aerodynamics: Recent Progress,* various papers and authors, SAE publication SP-855, 1991(b).

Samuelson, R. J. "Tinkering with Energy," *Newsweek,* March 4, 1991.

Santoro, S., et al. *Formaldehyde Emissions Control Technology for Methanol-Fueled Vehicles.* SAE Paper #902118, 1990.

Savitsky, D. "Hydrodynamic Design of Planing Hulls," *Marine Technology,* October 1964.

Savitsky, D. *On The Seakeeping of Planing Hulls.* SNAME paper presented May 26–28, 1966, Miami, Florida.

SCAQMD. *Annual Report, August 1990.* Southern California Air Quality Management District Technology Advancement Office, 1990.

SCAQMD. *1991 Air Quality Management Plan (Draft Final.* Southern California Association of Governments, 1991.

Scenic Hudson. *A Resource Book on Water-Saving Strategies for the 21st Century,* various papers presented at East-Meets-West Symposium, June 6, 1991.

Schmidt, Burt, Research and Development Engineer, Marine Power Inc., personal communication, 1992.

Schneider, K. "Thwarted Environmentalists Find U.S. Courts Are Citadels No More," *New York Times,* March 23, 1992.

Schuermann, D., et al. *Unregulated Motor Vehicle Exhaust Gas Components.* SAE Paper #902116, 1990.

Seideman, T. "The One-Lung Revolution," *Invention and Technology,* Winter, 1992.

Shemmans, M. J., et al. *NaS Batteries for Electric Vehicles.* SAE Paper #900136, 1990.

Shinozaki, O., et al. *Trapping Performance of Diesel Particulate Filters.* SAE Paper #900107, 1990.

Skorupa, J. "Coping with the New Gasolines," *Boating Industry,* February 1991.

Speltz, R. *The Real Runabouts. IV: Outboard Edition.* Lake Mills, IA: Graphic Publishing Co., 1982.

Steger, W., and J. Bowermaster. *Saving the Earth: A Citizen's Guide to Environmental Action.* New York: Knopf, 1990.

Steier, R. "Cleaner Fuel Means Gas Pains for City Drivers," *New York Post,* January 23, 1991.

Stobaugh, C. L., and R. Yergin (eds.). *Energy Future: Report of the Energy Project at the Harvard Business School.* New York: Vintage / Random House, 1983.

Teal, J.M., et al. "The West Falmouth Oil Spill After 20 Years: Fate of Fuel Oil Compounds and Effects on Animals," *Marine Pollution Bulletin,* vol. 24, number 12, 1992.

Thimsen, D. P., et al. *The Performance of an Electrostatic Agglomerator as a Diesel Soot Emission Control Device.* SAE Paper #900330, 1990.

Thomas, S. D. *The Last Navigator.* New York: Henry Holt, 1987.

Thompson, M. *Project Development Taking Shape.* Water Fuel Cell news release, Winter / Spring 1988–1989.

Thornton, Richard, Massachusetts Institute of Technology, personal communication, 1992.

Tilden, J. W., et al. *Effectiveness of Hydrocarbon Emission Controls in Rural Areas as an Ozone Strategy.* Prepared for OMC by Sierra Research, Sacramento, CA, 1991.

Tindall, Tom, Director of Two-Cycle Engineering, Detroit Diesel, Inc., personal communication, 1992.

Tripp, Bruce, Woods Hole Oceanographic Institute, personal communication, 1992.

United States Congress, Office of Technology Assessment. *Wastes in Marine Environments.* Washington, D.C.: Government Printing Office, 1986.

Verrier, R. "No More Sinking Feeling?" *Sarasota Herald-Tribune,* January 13, 1992.

Villiers, A. *Men, Ships, and the Sea.* Washington, D.C.: National Geographic Society, 1963.

von Westernhagen, H., et al. *Toxicity of Sea-Surface Microlayer: Effects on Herring and Turbot Embryos.* Marine Environmental Research #23, 1987.

Wald, M. L. "A Tough Sell for Electric Cars: Technology Lagging as Markets Emerge," *New York Times,* November 26, 1991.

Wald, M. L. "Cars that Whirr and Burn Rubber," *New York Times,* February 2, 1992.

Walker, J. "The Backyard Scientist: A Stirling Engine," *Scientific American,* January 1990.

Walton, F., et al. *Controlled Energy Deposition in Diesel Particulate Filters during Regeneration by Means of Microwave Irradiation.* SAE Paper #900327, 1990.

Weiss, Hilton, Professor of Chemistry, Bard College, personal communication, 1992.

Westdyk, K. "The Pacheco Generator Story," *The Messenger,* 1989.

Widdows, J., et al. *Physiological Responses of Mytilus Edulis during Chronic Oil Exposure and Recovery.* Marine Environmental Research #23, 1987.

Wills, R. "Future Storage: Hydrogen and Fuel Cells," abstract from the Northeast Sustainable Energy Association's abstract book of the Solar and Electric Vehicle Association Symposium, Manchester, NH, January 1991.

Wolfson, E. "Hazel Henderson: Re-Defining the Wealth of Nations," *E* magazine, September / October 1991.

Wouk, V. *Design of an E-Bus for Crosstown Operation on 42nd Street in New York City.* SAE Paper #900179, 1990.

Wuebben, P., et al. *The Future of Electric Vehicles in Meeting the Air Quality Challenges in Southern California.* SAE Paper #900580, 1990.

Yachting (no byline). "Times-Mirror / Roper Survey Results," July 1992, p. 12.

Zelenka, P., et al. *Reduction of Diesel Exhaust Emissions by Using Oxidation Catalysts.* SAE Paper #902111, 1990.

Index

acetylene, 94

acid rain, 34, 41, 58, 141, 200

aftercoolers, 145

air pollution:
California initiative on, 57–58, 96–97, 119, 132, 150
hydrocarbons in, 40-41, 62, 200–203
visible, 148
see also pollution

alcohol fuels, 94

Allen, Bryan, 188–89

Alternative Motor Fuels Act (1988), 99–100

aluminum, 180

aluminum-air batteries, 117, 118

American Public Transportation Association, 32

ammonia gas, 143

Amoco Cadiz oil spill, 46–47, 48

Analysis of Pollution from Marine Engines and Effects on the Environment, 58–61, 190

"Are the Seas Turning to Deserts?" (Pickthall), 37

Aronow, Don, 84, 85

Athens, Greece, trap oxidizers on buses in, 147–49, 150

automobiles:
alternators in, 108, 109, 114
design of, 71–72, 165–66, 186, 187
electric, 58, 68, 112–13, 119, 123, 150, 152
emission standards for, 31, 57–58, 138, 186, 195
energy efficiency of, 156
lobby for, 120
mass production of, 132
for middle class, 115–16, 132
mileage of, 30, 108, 109, 136, 138, 165
motorboats compared with, 30–33, 34, 71–72, 128–29, 133–34, 137, 138, 142, 185
number of, 77, 127
racing, 152
research and development (R&D) for, 118, 127–28, 132, 133
transmissions of, 156
use of, 142, 154

Axiak, V., 50

Baker, Charles, 112

Baldwin, Casey, 175

Bates, Marston, 192

batteries, 94, 107, 111–21
  for AC vs. DC motors, 151–52
  aluminum-air, 117, 118
  Edison's development of, 68, 112–
    14, 115, 118
  electricity for, 119–21, 162, 163
  energy density of, 150–51
  history of, 112–16
  lead-acid, 113, 114, 115, 116,
    117, 118, 153
  lithium ion, 115, 117, 118
  nickel-cadmium, 114, 115, 117
  nickel-iron, 114, 115, 116, 118
  nickel-zinc, 115, 116, 118
  production of, 114–15
  recent developments in, 116–21,
    162, 185
  silver-zinc, 117
  sodium-sulfur, 115, 116, 117, 118,
    136
  solar energy stored in, 110, 111–
    12
  types of, 116–17
  weight of, 151, 183
  zinc-air, 117, 118
Bell, Alexander Graham, 68, 175
Benz, Karl, 68, 130
benzene, 48, 97
Berrill, N. J., 192
Berthou, F., 46–47, 48
bicycle racing, 188
blacktop leachate, 41
boating, pleasure:
  environmental agenda for, 192–99
  history of, 64, 65–86
  as male activity, 86
  mentality of, 63, 75–76
  for middle class, 67
  popularity of, 11, 65, 83–84
  product failures in, 70–71
  sailboats for, 66–67, 163
  sensible, 181–82
  see also motorboats; pollution; spe-
    cific topics
boating industry:
  cost reduction in, 69, 70
  employment in, 62
  EPA and, 52, 58–61, 62, 195
  founders of, 68
  government regulation of, 135,
    193, 194–97
  marketing in, 71–72, 75

  military contracts of, 69
  rationalizations used by, 67, 158
  research and development (R&D)
    in, 133–34, 182, 190, 195; see
    also design, boat
  shows held by, 71–72
  taxation and, 35, 194, 195
Boating Industry, 19–20
Boating Industry Associaton, 52, 58–
    61
boats:
  in air-water interface, 44–46, 166
  aluminum, 180
  duty cycles of, 26, 27, 86, 154
  efficiency ratings for, 178–81,
    182, 196
  fiberglass, 69–70, 77, 155
  financing for, 72
  low-resistance, 164, 165–90
  as nonroad vehicles, 28, 62
  outdated, 195
  "perfect," 68, 166
  planing, 173–76
  sex appeal and, 85–86
  stability of, 189–90
  wooden, 69, 78–79, 80, 81, 126
  see also design, boat; motorboats;
    sailboats
BOC Challenge (1990), 36–37
Brown, Samuel, 128–29
brushless DC propulsion, 152
Bulkeley, John, 78–79
buses, 102–3, 105, 108–9, 143,
    147–49, 150, 165
Bush, George, 100
butane, 97

California, emission levels allowed
    in, 57–58, 96–97, 119, 132,
    150
cancer, 11, 40, 43, 49, 202
carbon, 94, 194
carbon dioxide, 46, 96, 101, 141,
    162
carbon monoxide, 96, 140–41, 147,
    162
carbon tetrachloride, 202
Carson, Rachel, 192, 203
catalytic converters, 31, 96, 97, 98,
    127, 133, 140–42, 147, 161,
    165, 183, 184

catamarans, 125–26, 167, 168, 177, 180, 183
Catskill Waters, 13
cerium naphthenate, 149
cetane, 103
chlorine, 202, 203
chlorofluorocarbons, 200–201
chloroform, 203
Chmura, G. L., 46
Chris-Craft, 17, 68, 80, 81
chromosome damage, 49, 52–53
Chrysler, 118, 135, 136
Churchill, Winston S., 77
Cigarette, 85
clean air legislation, 52, 97, 116, 132
Clearwater, 12, 22
Cleopatra's Barge, 67
Clerk, Dugald, 129–30
coal:
    burning of, 127–28
    dust from, 144
    gas from, 106, 128–29
    ships powered by, 77
Coates, S. W., 28
cocaine, 85
Columbian Exposition (1893), 153
Columbus, Christopher, 167, 201
Cook, James, 167, 168, 170
copepods, 36, 50
Corner, N., 47, 51
crabs, 44, 52
crankcases, 132, 135
Cross, J. N., 49, 51, 202–3
crosswinds, 188, 189
Crouch, George, 74
Crowninshield, George, Jr., 67
cruisers, 182, 183–84
Curzon, George Nathaniel, Lord, 77

Daimler, Gottlieb, 68, 129, 130
Daimler-Benz Corporation, 130–31
Daniels, Josephus, 91
DDT, 202, 203
design, boat, 165–91
    aerodynamics of, 186–90
    automobile design as influence on, 71–72
    development of, 166–68
    energy efficiency and, 25, 163–64, 178–81, 182, 196
    hydrodynamics of, 165–86
    for racing, 72–77

streamlined, 186–87, 189
    see also boats; hulls
Deterding, Henri, 91, 92
Detroit Diesel Corporation (DDC), 98, 146
Dickens, Charles, 128
Diesel, Rudolf, 143–44
diesel engines, 143–50
    cost of, 145, 147
    emisson standards for, 102–3, 146, 147–50
    exhaust from, 22, 143, 146, 161–62
    gas-fueled, 104, 147
    generators powered by, 122, 184
    horsepower of, 144–45, 146
    invention of, 143–44
    marine, 145, 146
    methanol-fueled, 98, 146–47
    trap oxidizers for, 147–49, 184
    two-stroke, 145–46
diesel fuel:
    gasoline vs., 145
    hydrocarbons in, 94, 102–3
    reformulated, 147, 162
    as type of oil, 39, 42, 144, 145
DNA, 53
docking, 189, 190
Dodge, Horace, 69, 72
Doolittle, Jimmy, 79
Drake, Edward, 89, 129
dynamometers, 137

East is a Big Bird (Gladwin), 56
EBDI (external breathing direct injection), 129–30, 136, 161
Edison, Thomas A., 68, 112–14, 115, 118
Edward I, King of England, 128
"Elastic Trawler, The" (Fxas), 181
Elco, 69, 80, 151, 181, 182
electrical switches, 70–71
electric automobiles, 58, 68, 112–13, 119, 123, 150, 152
electric motorboats, 67–68, 119, 120–21, 150–55, 182, 184–85
electrolysis, 108, 109
electrostatic agglomerators, 149–50
Elizabeth Watts, 90
emission standards, 27–29, 31, 41, 57–58, 62, 96–97, 102–3,

emission standards (*continued*)
119, 132, 135–42, 146, 147–
50, 186, 195, 196
emphysema, 11, 40
energy, 87–124
conservation of, 120
conversion of, 121–22, 163
efficient use of, 25, 155–58, 159,
163–64, 178–81, 182, 187,
196
solar, 14, 17–25, 107, 109–12,
183
types of, 87–124
see also fuel
engine management system (EMS),
133, 139–40, 142, 143, 148,
154, 161, 162, 196
engines:
aftercoolers for, 145
backpressure on, 142, 148
big- vs. small-block, 136–37
clean combustion by, 139–40,
165, 194, 197, 198
Clerk-cycle, 129–30
conversion of, 104
developments in, 127–33
displacement by, 74
dual-fuel, 100, 104–5
efficiency of, 133–38, 151
four-stroke, 27, 129, 136, 137–38,
145, 146, 161, 183
fuel-injected, 31, 133, 138–39,
161
government specifications for,
127–28
gunpowder-fueled, 128
horsepower of, 59, 74, 75–82,
131, 134, 144–45, 146
inboard, 29
internal combustion (IC), 67, 88,
89, 90, 112, 113–16, 119–20,
121, 122, 123, 127–33, 138,
143, 150, 151, 162
noise of, 62–63, 162
oil-injected, 135
one-lunger, 131–32
periodic inspections of, 196–97
power-to-weight ratio for, 137,
146
practicability of, 133
propulsion for, 87, 88, 89, 123–
24, 150–55, 162, 197

for racing, 67, 74, 76
recommendations for, 160–63
refinement of, 127–28
speed ranges of, 86, 134
steam, 128, 129, 131
sterndrive, 29, 31, 76, 156, 157,
159, 161
straight-4, 132–33
total loss lubrication of, 136
turbocharged, 31, 138, 139, 145,
161, 162
two-stroke, 26–29, 31, 39, 62,
129–30, 131–32, 135–36,
145–46, 161, 194, 198
V-6, 31, 132–33, 135, 138
V-8, 31, 76, 132, 134–35, 137,
138
variable-speed, 130, 154, 163
water-cooled, 133
weight of, 74, 136, 137, 161
see also diesel engines; outboard
motors
environment:
ecological balance in, 14, 101
government involvement in, 194–
97
individual involvement in, 197–98
see also pollution
Environmental Protection Agency
(EPA):
boating industry and, 52, 58–61,
62, 195
emissions data of, 27–28, 41, 62
motorboat pollution studied by,
58–61, 190
oil industry and, 95
oxygenated fuels supported by, 96
shellfish beds closed by, 45
EPA PB92-126960 report, 62
ethanol, 94, 98, 99, 100–101, 121,
142, 163
EVs (electric vehicles), 119, 120
exhaust:
aquatic life "stimulated" by, 58,
60
dampening of, 63
dedicated stroke for, 27
diesel, 22, 143, 146, 161–62
emission standards for, 57–58,
96–97, 119, 132, 135–42,
150, 196
engine out, 142

gas recirculation for, 139
from outboard motors, 26–29, 39, 62
particulates in, 28, 104, 147–49
wet, 133, 141–42, 161
Exxon Valdez oil spill, 20, 21, 29, 33, 35–36

Fexas, Tom, 181–82
fiberglass, 69–70, 77, 155
fish, 36, 43, 45, 48, 49, 52
fishing, 26, 30, 59, 171
fishing trolling motors, 153
flame-quenching, 139
Fleming, Joe, 151
Florida, 42
Ford, Henry, 68, 69, 72, 112, 113–14, 132, 201
Ford, Henry, II, 107
Ford Model N, 113–14
Ford Motor Company, 105, 118, 132, 135, 136
formaldehyde, 100, 147
four-stroke engines, 27, 129, 136, 137–38, 145, 146, 161, 183
Freon, 200, 202
fuel:
  alcohol, 94, 98–102
  batteries compared with, 121, 150–51
  increased consumption of, 75–76
  lean burning of, 96
  oxygenated, 96, 97–98
  reduced consumption of, 25, 134–38, 144, 198
  shadow factor for, 32, 34
  social impact of, 87–88
  tax on, 195
  types of, 89–109
  waste of, 22–25, 29–30, 191
  see also specific fuels
fuel cells (FCs), 94, 105, 106, 108, 121–24, 154
fuel-injected engines, 31, 133, 138–39, 161

gallium arsenide crystal, 111
Gardiner, W. W., 45, 52
Gar Wood, 71, 74
gas, ammonia, 143
gas, natural, 121, 142

compressed (CNG), 103–5, 147, 163
distribution of, 104, 105, 122
liquid (LNG), 104, 105, 142
as petroleum-derived, 93, 94
storage of, 105
see also fuel
gasoline, 95–98, 106, 128–29, 144
  blends of, 95
  diesel fuel vs., 145
  energy density of, 150–51
  hydrocarbons in, 95, 96–97
  cracking process for, 95, 102
  octane ratings of, 97, 99
  for outboard motors, 20, 26, 27, 28–29, 39
  as petroleum-derived, 94, 95
  price of, 97–98, 99, 104
  production of, 77
  reformulated, 97–98, 102
  social cost per gallon of, 35
  super unleaded, 99
  see also fuel
General Motors (GM), 105, 118, 132, 135, 152
generators, 122, 154, 184
George, J. J., 50
Georgetown University, 123
German, John, 136
Gladwin, Thomas, 56
Good Times Too, 22–25
Gossamer Albatross, 188–89
greenhouse effect, 96, 100
Greenpeace, 35–36
Gulf War, 21, 40

Hard Times (Dickens), 128
Hardy, John T., 41, 45, 49–51, 203
Harvard Business School, 192
Hatfield, Roger, 177
Henry the Navigator, Prince of Portugal, 168
herring, 48, 52
Hindenburg disaster, 108
Hitler, Adolf, 78
hot rods, 134–35
hovercraft, 169, 176
Hoyt, Garry, 175–76
hulls:
  design of, 87, 164, 166–68
  displacement, 88, 170–72, 180–81

hulls (*continued*)
drag of, 172, 175, 177, 178, 187, 188, 189
lift of, 172
limiting speed of, 170–71, 173
mono-, 168, 181
multi-, 125–26, 167, 168–70, 180, 181
penetrating, 169–70, 177–78, 180, 181
planing, 173–74
racing, 174
resistance of, 25, 88, 154, 157, 164, 166, 168–70, 173, 196
semi-planing, 172–73, 180, 181
semi-submersible, 177
skin friction of, 171, 173, 174, 177
speed of, 170–72, 173, 181
stepped, 174
V-bottom, 75, 88, 176
wave motion and, 22–24, 166, 169–170, 171, 172, 175, 177, 178
weight distribution of, 169
Huygens, Christiaan, 128
hydrocarbons:
air pollution from, 40–41, 200–203
from automobiles vs. motorboats, 32, 34
as carcinogenic, 43, 49, 202
chemical composition of, 39, 42, 94, 201–2
chlorinated, 200–203
chromosome damage from, 49, 52–53
concentrations of, 48–50
emission levels for, 95, 96–97, 102–3, 123, 135, 136, 138–40, 141, 160, 191, 196
fuel waste and, 29–30
hormones mimicked by, 53
invisibility of, 11, 30–31, 40
from land runoff, 41, 46
metabolic rates and, 59
as morphogenic, 43, 49–50, 52
as mutagenic, 42–43, 49
in oil, 39, 42, 43, 89
from outboard motors, 26, 27, 28, 29, 31, 39
photoreactivity of, 40, 43, 62

polycyclic aromatic (PAH), 42–43, 47, 48, 103, 143
in stressed ponds, 59–61
as teratogenic, 43, 49
hydrodynamics, 165–86
hydrofoils, 68, 174–76
hydrogen, 94, 105–9, 110, 136
hydroplanes, 74, 75
stepped, 174
three-point, 174

ignition:
compression, 98, 100, 142, 143–45, 161
electronic, 31, 103, 127, 130
spark, 143, 145, 161, 163
inboard engines, 29
industrial revolution, 127–28
insurance, boat, 163, 197
internal combustion (IC) engines, 67, 88, 89, 90, 112, 113–16, 119–20, 121, 122, 123, 127–33, 138, 143, 150, 151, 162

Jamais Contente electric car, 112
Jenatzy, Camille, 112, 150
jets, fighter, 30
joyriding, 18–19, 21, 26

Kennedy, John F., 79
Kier, Samuel, 89
Kocan, R. M., 48, 49, 51
kyphosis, 49

LaHage, Barbara S., 56–57
Lassanske, G. G., 28
launches, 69, 151, 171, 179
solar, 14, 17–25
Lawrence Livermore Laboratory, 120
lead-acid batteries, 113, 114, 115, 116, 117, 118, 153
Lee, V., 52
Lenoir, Pierre, 90, 129
lithium ion batteries, 115, 117, 118
lobsters, 52, 131
lordosis, 50
Lorenzen, John, 107–8
Los Angeles, air pollution in, 32–33
Lovins, Amory, 63–64
Lovins, Hunter, 63

McCoy, Bill, 84
MacReady, Paul, 117
magazines, boating, 80, 196, 197
Marconi, Guglielmo, 68
Marcus, Siegfried, 90, 129
marinas, 77, 163, 195
Marinoni, Hippolyte, 129
Massachusetts:
  alcohol fuels used in, 99
  emission levels allowed in, 119,
    150
Massachusetts Water Resource
    Authority, 56–57
Maybach, Wilhelm, 130
Mazda rotary engine, 137
Mediterranean Sea, 29
methane, 103, 123, 147, 201–2
methanol, 94, 98, 99, 101, 121, 142,
    146–47, 163
methyl chloride, 202
Meyer, Stan, 107
microwave irradiation, 149
Midnight Lace cruisers, 182
Milliken, A. S., 52
MLs (armed motor launches), 69
mollusks, 50
motorboats:
  air resistance for, 187–89
  automobiles compared with, 30–
    33, 34, 71–72, 128–29, 133–
    34, 137, 138, 142, 185
  concentrations of, 31, 59
  efficient technology for, 63–64,
    82, 87, 88, 178–86, 190
  electric, 67–68, 119, 120–21,
    150–55, 182, 184–85
  electrical systems of, 110
  emission standards for, 31, 33,
    58–61, 119, 190, 194
  interiors of, 82–84
  invention of, 128–29
  lemon laws for, 62
  length of, 74
  market for, 68, 71–72, 74, 75
  mileage of, 30, 137, 178, 179
  noise controls for, 62–63
  number of, 20, 25–26, 28, 126–27
  planing by, 76
  price of, 133
  production of, 69–71, 73, 75, 77
  sales figures for, 20, 40, 62, 75,
    85–86, 142–43

speed limit legislation for, 63
torque requirements of, 134, 137,
    143, 162, 164
transmissions of, 156–57, 163
velocity of, 88
weight of, 83
see also outboard motors; *specific
    types of motorboats*
motorcycles, 135
muriatic acid, 109
mussels, 43, 47
Mussolini, Benito, 78

naphtha, 98, 102
National Aeronautics and Space
    Administration (NASA), 108
National Marine Manufacturers
    Association (NMMA), 20
  environmental policy of, 61–63,
    190, 196, 197, 198
neuston, 45
New York:
  alcohol fuels used in, 99
  gasoline prices in, 97–98, 104
  water reservoirs in, 12–13
New York Post, 97
nickel-cadmium batteries, 114, 115,
    117
nickel-iron batteries, 114, 115, 116,
    118
nickel-zinc batteries, 115, 116, 118
nitrogen, 40
nitrogen oxides, 62, 96, 103, 106,
    123, 136, 141, 143, 147, 162
noise pollution, 19, 62–63, 162

oceans:
  as deserts, 36–37, 203
  environmental importance of, 13–
    14
  food chain in, 36, 45, 48-49
  see also water pollution
Ogden, Joan, 110
oil:
  crude, 39, 42, 43, 52
  as diesel fuel, 39, 42, 144, 145
  economic growth and, 36
  environmental impact of, 41–55,
    191
  grades of, 39
  heating, 39, 42
  hydrocarbons in, 39, 42, 43, 89

oil (*continued*)
  industry for, 89–94, 95
  lubricating, 20–21, 26, 28, 39, 90,
    136, 140
  pipelines for, 90–91, 92
  price of, 119
  production of, 89–94, 109
  Rule of Capture for, 92, 94
  shipment of, 90
  strategic importance of, 21, 35,
    77–78, 110
  supplies of, 34–35, 91–94
  U.S. dependence on, 82, 83, 98,
    99, 101, 103, 192
  see also fuel
oil-injected engines, 135
oil spills:
  Amoco Cadiz, 46–47, 48
  Exxon Valdez, 20, 21, 29, 33, 35–
    36
  West Falmouth, 42–44
OMC, 81–82, 135
Orbital engine, 136, 161
Otto, Nicholas, 68, 129
outboard motors:
  catalytic converters for, 161
  development of, 68
  emissions data on, 27–29
  exhaust from, 26–29, 39, 62
  four-stroke, 161, 183
  gasoline used by, 20, 26, 27, 28–
    29, 39
  hydrocarbon emissions from, 26,
    27, 28, 29, 31, 39
  lubricating oil spilled by, 20–21,
    26, 28, 39
  noise from, 19
  older, 28
  ports of, 27
  propellers for, 156, 157
  for racing, 76
  sales figures for, 20, 28
  steady-state operation of, 28
  two-stroke, 26–29, 31, 39, 62,
    135, 161, 194, 198
  V-6, 135
  V-8, 135
  see also motorboats
oxides of nitrogen, 62, 96, 103, 106,
  123, 136, 141, 143, 147, 162
oysters, 44, 47, 48
ozone hole, 200–201

Pacheco, Francisco, 106
panels, solar, 110–11, 183
Pattas, K., 148
Patton, George S., 79
PCBs (polychlorinated biphenyls),
  48, 58
photovoltaics, 110, 111
Pickthall, B., 37
plankton, 36, 46, 50
pleasure boating, *see* boating, pleasure
Podolny, William, 122
pollution:
  from automobiles vs. motorboats,
    30–33
  low-level, 49, 51, 53–54
  noise, 19, 62–63, 162
  pervasiveness of, 54–55
  social costs of, 33–35
  see also air pollution; water pollu-
    tion; *specific topics*
ponds, stressed, 59–61
pontoon boats, 180
powerboats, *see* motorboats
power plants, 119–20, 122, 163
Prince William Sound, 40, 46
proas, 168
propane, 104
propellers, 155–60, 180
  cavitation by, 157–58, 159
  counter-rotating, 184
  energy efficiency of, 155–58, 159,
    187, 196
  improved design of, 158–60, 163,
    179, 184
  laminar flow of, 158
  for outboard motors, 156, 157
  size of, 157–58, 159
  tip vortices of, 158
  turbofan, 159
  turbulence from, 29
  variable-pitch, 159–60, 163
propulsion systems, 87, 88, 89, 123–
  24, 150–55, 162, 197
PT boats, 78–79, 80, 81
Puget Sound, 45, 49–50, 52–53, 203
pulse-width-modulation systems,
  153
Puluwat Atoll seamen, 56
pumps, water, 128

quarter wave, 170, 173

racing:
  boat design influenced by, 72–77
  engines for, 67, 74, 76
  hulls for, 174
  offshore, 74–75
  speed in, 74–76
racing automobiles, 152
rain, acid, 34, 41, 58, 141, 200
Ramus, Reverend, 174
Reagan, Ronald, 82
Rockefeller, John D., 91, 92, 144
Rocky Mountain Institute, 63
Rommel, Erwin, 79
rooting, 170
Ross, N. W., 46
rowboats, 171
Royal Dutch Shell, 91–92
Royal Navy, 77
rudders, 188
rumrunners, 84–85
runabouts, 18–19, 26, 30, 70, 72,
  146, 180, 184
Rural Electricification Administration, 107

sailboats:
  air resistance for, 188
  gaff-rigged, 22
  hull speeds of, 171–72
  industry for, 182
  multihull, 125–26, 167
  for pleasure boating, 66–67, 163
  racing by, 73
  training on, 22
  wind power for, 125–26
sand dollars, 52, 53
Santayana, George, 64
Sargasso Sea, 45
scoliosis, 50
sea turtles, 45
shellfish, 36, 45
Silent Spring (Carson), 203
silver-zinc batteries, 117
Sintz, Clark, 130
Smith, Chris, 68
Smith, Roger, 107
smog, 11, 34, 40, 62, 96, 103, 141,
  201
Society of Automotive Engineers, 27
sodium chloride, 202
sodium-sulfur batteries, 115, 116,
  117, 118, 136

Solar Challenger, 117
solar energy, 110–12
  abundance of, 109
  author's use of, 14, 17–25, 111
  collectors for, 110–11, 183
  heating by, 107
  storage of, 110, 111–12
soot, 148, 149–50
spark plugs, 104, 139
speed:
  cruising, 130, 134, 137, 154
  efficiency and, 178, 179
  in electric propulsion systems,
    153, 154
  hull, 170–72, 173, 181
  low, 162–63, 184–86, 198
  as post-war legacy, 77–82, 86
  in racing, 74–76
  ranges of, 86, 134
speedometers, 76
Standard Oil, 91–92, 119
steam engines, 128, 129, 131
steamships, 90
steering wheels, 71
Steinway, William, 130–31
sterndrive engines, 29, 31, 76, 156,
  157, 159, 161
stern wave, 170, 173
straight-4 engines, 132–33
Street, Robert, 128
submarines, 177
sulfur, 103, 162
sulfur oxides, 41, 46
SWATH, 177
switches, electrical, 70–71

tainting, 52
tankers, 24, 34–35, 45–46, 145
technology-forcing, 127–28, 132,
  133, 142, 146, 153, 160
temperature inversions, 96
thermal inertia, 123
tidal marshes, 43–44, 45, 46, 54
TLEVs (transitional low-emission
  vehicles), 150
toilets, low-flow, 57
trailers, boat, 77
trap oxidizers, 147–49, 150, 184
trawler yachts, 171, 179, 180
trimarans, 177
trout streams, 12–13
trucks, 103, 104, 146, 165

tugboats, 171
turbines, wind, 126
turbocharged engines, 31, 138, 139, 145, 161, 162
turbot, 49
turpentine, 128
Twenty Thousand Leagues Under the Sea (Verne), 106
two-stroke engines, 26–29, 31, 39, 62, 129–30, 131–32, 135–36, 145–46, 161, 194, 198

ULEVs (ultra-low emission vehicles), 150
Unique Mobility, 152
Unocal program, 195
upholstery, 71, 83

V-6 engines, 31, 132–33, 135, 138
V-8 engines, 31, 76, 132, 134–35, 137, 138
Van Blerck, Joe, 74
variable-pitch propellers, 159–60, 163
variable-speed engines, 130, 154, 163
Verne, Jules, 106
Vienna Exposition (1875), 129
Vietnam War, 21
volatile organic compounds (VOC), 62
von Westernhagen, H., 49, 51

Wagman, Art, 105
walking, 30
Wallace, Henry, 106
Watercars, 72
water-cooled engines, 133
water pollution:
   aquatic life destroyed by, 35–37, 43–55
   bathtub-ring effect of, 44–45, 52
   contamination by, 47–53
   evidence of, 36–39, 47
   extinction from, 14, 37, 49, 50, 51–52, 54, 203
   fates of, 48
   in fresh vs. salt water, 41, 44
   fuel waste and, 24–25, 29–30

   hydrocarbons in, 41–55, 59–60
   invisibility of, 11, 29, 39–40, 43, 50–51
   long-term effects of, 42, 43–44, 47–48, 59, 61
   microlayer affected by, 36, 44–46, 51, 54, 59, 166
   reproductive cycle affected by, 36, 42–43, 44, 45, 48, 49, 50–51, 52–53
   scientific investigation of, 54–55, 58–61
   social costs of, 33–35, 87–88, 141, 193
   near urban areas, 49
   see also pollution
water-skiing, 26, 59
water taxis, 88
weather patterns, 36
West Falmouth (Mass.) oil spill, 42–44
whale sharks, 45
Widdows, J., 47
windmills, 107
wind power, 125–26
wind pressure, 187
Wisconsin, University of, 26, 27, 28, 86
Woods Hole Oceanographic Institute, 42
Woody Guthrie, 22
World War I, 77–78
World War II, 78–79, 94
Wright, Orville and Wilbur, 68

Yachting, 36–37
yachts:
   commuter, 71
   development of, 66–67
   fuel wasted by, 22–25
   interiors of, 82–83
   royal, 66
   trawler, 171, 179, 180
   wake of, 22–24
Yeager, Chuck, 79

ZEVs (zero-emission vehicles), 119–20, 150
zinc-air batteries, 117, 118